Silent No More

Women in Ministry Reclaiming the Leader Within

Edited by Dr. Mae Alice Reggy

The Story Behind the Book

In 2009, I had the opportunity to teach a course on *Women in Theology* in the graduate program at Beulah Heights University. The course was concerned with the role of women in ministry from an historical, liturgical, theological, and cultural perspective. Course materials selected were geared toward helping students develop a holistic biblical hermeneutic of male-female relationships and ministry roles. My aspirations for this course were to equip students to deal with the issue of biblical equality from an informed position.

It was a modular course consisting of six intensive classroom sessions, augmented by pre- and post-class assignments. The classroom sessions were conducted on Friday evenings and all-day Saturdays during the months of October, November and December. Pre-class work included reading textbooks, such as *Women in the Church* (Grenz and Kjesbo)[1] dealing with the historical global perspective of women in ministry; also *Beyond Sex Roles* (Bilezikian)[2] and *Women in Ministry* (Clouse and Clouse)[3] dealing with the exegesis of biblical passages related to male-female leadership. During the classroom sessions, students discussed the readings and presented papers. Additionally, they viewed DVDs, including *Every Soldier Counts* and *Women of*

---

[1] Stanley J. Grenz and Denise Muir Kjesbo, *Women in the Church: A Biblical Theology of Women in Ministry* (Downers Grove: InterVarsity Press, 1995).

[2] Gilbert Bilezikian, *Beyond Sex Roles: What the Bible Says about a Woman's Place in Church and Family* (Grand Rapids: Baker Publishing Group, 2006).

[3] Bonnidell Clouse and Robert G. Clouse, *Women in Ministry: Four Views* (Downers Grove: InterVarsity Press, 1989).

Azusa Street. At the end of the course, the students were encouraged to discuss their personal theology and attitude concerning women in ministry and apply that attitude within the context of contemporary church structure.

In total, eleven students enrolled in the course—ten women and one man. All were outstanding students. In my estimation, they were the cream of the crop. All had earned their Bachelor of Arts Degree and are now pursuing post-graduate degrees. All were involved in ministry either as pastors, evangelists, church planters, missionaries or lay-leaders. Each of them had a unique story to tell. As a post-class assignment, they agreed to write their own personal stories to inspire thousands of voiceless women who are being denied their rightful role in the church. Together, we would publish a book so that those coming behind them will benefit from their experiences in life and ministry. To this end, the students began to narrate their stories, answering such questions as: What events and circumstances led to their call to ministry? What are some of the challenges they deal with as women in ministry? What are their aspirations for the future?

As the writing process dragged on, four women students declined to be a part of the book project but one of my former students—also a Beulah Heights University graduate—joined in. The one male wrote a very moving article on male-female roles, but declined to submit it for publication. In the end, eight students submitted articles. This book, *Silent No More* is a result of their reflections on their often times tumultuous journey as women called to ministry. I intentionally kept editing of these articles to a minimum, so that the reader will hear the authentic voices of these eight outstanding women who are reclaiming the leader within.

Acknowledgements
Special thanks are due

To Dr. Angelita Howard and Dr. Anyango E. Reggy for their contribution to this book.

To Dr. Toni Alvarado, Mrs. Joyce Latson, Dr. Chyanna Mull-Anthony, and Dr. Betty Palmer for their endorsements.

To Mr. Marcelo Silva for designing the cover and layout of this book.

To Evelyn Bell, Marilyn Maye, Ebony Moore, and Judy Rae Kirk for offering their advice at various stages of this project.

To Beverly Ponder, Christine Hameed, Natalie Brannon-Lipede, Patricia Jones, Rebecca Manning, T.G. Monroy, and Wanda Crowder for their courage to share their joys and sorrows.

Content

Forward

Women are entering the ministry in significant numbers either as ordained ministers or leaders of certain ministries. Over the years, we have seen a major shift in the roles that women play in the church. For years, women have struggled and continue to struggle with being leaders and working with men and in dealing with the "hierarchy of denominations."

Ninety two years ago...

The late Reverend Paul T. Barth, and his wife, Dr. Hattie M. Barth, founded Beulah Heights Bible Institute in 1918. The driving force bringing the school into being was Mrs. Elizabeth A. Sexton, Mrs. Barth's mother. Mrs. Sexton, also known as "Mother Sexton," communicated her vision of a Pentecostal Bible School in Atlanta, Georgia to others. The school restricted itself to working with a few local students until 1928.

After 1928, the outreach of the school expanded and new buildings were added. In 1940, Beulah Heights Institute of Atlanta and Southeastern Bible Institute of New Brockton, Alabama combined to become the Beulah-Heights-Southeastern Bible Institute in Atlanta, Georgia. In 1962, the name of the school was changed to Beulah Heights College, Seminary and Institute, thus establishing a four-year Bible College. In 2006, the name was changed to Beulah Heights University. The university now serves approximately 815 students from over 38 countries, and offers graduate programs leading to the Masters in Religious Studies, Masters in Leadership Studies, Masters of Divinity, and Masters in Business Administration. Also, the university has satellite programs in Griffin, Georgia and Brazil. Talks are underway to establish satellites in Kenya and South Korea as well.

Through the years, our institution has offered quality education to those in the Atlanta community and abroad. A high-quality Christian education prepares students—male and female—for service and leadership in ministry and marketplace. Courses are offered in array of formats: to accommodate all students—their learning styles, and their busy lives. At Beulah Heights University, instructors as well as students, consider it their responsibility to have a whole-soul (mind, will and emotion) encounter with God. Not only do instructors teach, they also continually dig into the Scriptures to seek the wisdom of God.

In her book titled *Leading Women*, Carol Becker addresses issues concerning the rapidly growing number of women in positions of church leadership. She says "no matter what position they hold, women in church leadership cite the invisibility traps as the most common and perhaps the most frustrating." These traps have much to do with the woman not being seen, or if seen, rarely at all. At Beulah Heights, we support women in leadership as pastors, teachers, chaplains, lay persons and so on. Courses such as *Exploring Gender Differences*, *Women in Leadership*, and *Women in Theology* are designed to enhance certain skill assets in women and men. As it now stands, approximately fifty-two percent of our students at Beulah Heights University are female, and women serve in many capacities, from Vice President to Department Chair to Instructors. We have outstanding women leaders on our board of directors and our weekly chapel speakers include pastors and preachers from all over the world; many of them are women.

I am excited about *Silent No More* as this book is a compilation of female student work lead by Dr. Mae Alice Reggy. She has done a phenomenal job of exploring gender differences and capturing the pure essence of women in leadership in ministry and marketplace. I do believe this book will encourage and give hope to those women who have battled and struggled against obstacles in life to achieve a place in ministry. Women, I believe it is our time to reclaim the leader within. Journey through this book, and be Silent No More! I leave you with a quote from a simple but powerful speech by Sojourner Truth, delivered in 1851 at the Women's Convention in Akron, Ohio:

> Well children, where there is so much racket there must be something out of kilter. That man over there says that women need to be helped into carriages, and lifted over ditches, and to have the best place everywhere. Nobody ever helps me into carriages, or over mud-puddles, or give me any best place! And ain't I a woman?

> Look at me! Look at my arm! I have ploughed and planted, and gathered into barns, and no man could help me! And ain't I a woman?

> I could work as much and eat as much as a man-when I could get it-and bear the lash as well! And ain't I a woman?

> I have borne thirteen children, and seen most all sold off to slavery, and when I cried out with my mother's grief, none but Jesus heard me! And ain't I a woman?

> Then that little man in black there, he says women can't have as much rights as men, 'cause Christ wasn't a woman! Where did your Christ come from? Where

did your Christ come from? From God and a Woman! Man had nothing to do with Him.

If the first woman God ever made was strong enough to turn the world upside down all alone, these women together ought to be able to turn it back, and get it right side up again! And now they are asking to do it, the men better let them.

Now ain't I a woman!

Dr. Angelita Howard
Beulah Heights University
Vice President of Institutional Effectiveness & Planning

PART 1

Introduction

"The Church has managed to silence women over the centuries and promotes their secondary position in the name of the Scriptures, church tradition, and socio-cultural context. Is today's church willing to make a difference? Are women willing to take risks to ensure life by challenging the structures of death? It is easy to enjoy our comforts, avail church benefits, and remain silent. It is difficult to walk the way of the cross, challenging the unjust structures as Christ did. But that is the only way for life eternal."

Prasanna Kumari
Women's Participation and Contribution to the Church

Looking Back, Moving Ahead
By Mae Alice Reggy

During the 1930's, my dad migrated from Valdosta, Georgia and found work under a series of economic programs passed by Congress in response to the Great Depression. My mom journeyed from Lynchburg, Virginia in the 1940's to stay with her elder sister who worked in the Picatinny Arsenal. During World War II, Picatinny was a major plant developing weapons and munitions. They married and settled in northern New Jersey where my brother and I were born.

My parent's generation was raised in an uncertain socio-economic environment with few safety nets. They told me how large numbers of African-Americans migrated from the South desperate to find jobs and support their families. They toiled as day laborers so that their children could have a better future. Their generation found meaning in traditional values and instilled in their children the importance of "keeping one's word", "maintaining one's good name" and so on. They had respect for authority and seemed comfortable with hierarchical organizational structures. Although women made up the largest percentage of the population as a whole, men were given higher authority in the workplace. This was consistent with the values of their generation in which generally men were expected to be the primary wage earners and women entered the workforce to "help out" their families or the nation during times of crisis such as World War II.

By the time, I was old enough to remember, my dad was already an ordained minister and serving as an unsalaried associate pastor in a small (then storefront) church. I remember how he loved to read the Bible; he called himself a "read on" preacher. In church meetings, he would read a long passage of biblical text and then explicate it so clearly that even a child could understand. My mom loved the Bible and she could preach too but she rarely got the chance. Although the majority of church members were women, our denomination (and many others) did not believe in women preachers. My parent's generation saw women enter the workforce and confront issues of racial and gender equality at work, but the Church kept women marginalized, powerless, silent with little or no opportunities to use their gifts and abilities. Women could teach Sunday school or speak in the women's meetings, but they could not be ordained or even preach on Sunday mornings. Thus, church women remained in the background, cooking chicken dinners, sewing choir robes, and "helping" male leaders.

By working hard and saving, my parents were able to give me better opportunities than they had. Growing up, I would often hear church folks speak disparagingly about education-"*the letter killeth*" they'd say. But during my teen years, a progressive young preacher, Rev. Kelmo Porter Jr. who had just graduated from New York University was appointed senior pastor. He inspired me to achieve academic excellence. After graduating from high school, I entered Douglass College, Rutgers University and earned a Bachelor of Arts degree. Inspired by President John F. Kennedy's words spoken on January 20, 1961—"Ask not what your country can do for you - ask what you can do for your country"— I joined the U.S. Peace Corps two months after college graduation and served two years as a teacher in northern Turkey. On returning to the

United States, I joined the Urban Teacher Corps, taught in an inner-city school and earned a Masters Degree from Howard University, and a Ph.D. from University of Maryland.

Looking back, I realize that my generation grew up genuinely expecting the world to improve with time. We witnessed and participated in some of the greatest social changes in the nation's history: the Environmental Movement, the Women's Movement, and the Civil Rights Movement. As a young person, I took part in the celebrated March on Washington on August 28, 1963 and was among over 200,000 civil rights supporters there in front of the Lincoln Memorial when Dr. Martin Luther King Jr. delivered his poignant "I Have a Dream" speech. In May 1968, I witnessed the Poor People's March organized by Dr. King where—after his assassination—thousands of poor people of all races set up a shantytown on the grounds of the Washington Monument to protest racism and poverty in the United States.

Although income differences remained and poverty increased among minorities, there were dramatic shifts in educational, economic and social opportunities. With shifts in the marketplace from a paternalistic, racially homogeneous environment to one of increased gender and racial equality, my generation coined terms like the "glass ceiling" and "equal opportunity workplace."[4] With all of the social changes, the churches still managed to silence women and promote their secondary position in the name of the Scriptures, church tradition, and socio-cultural context.[5]

---

[4] (No Author given), "Managing a Multigenerational Workforce, The Diversity Manager's Toolkit," Cook Ross, Inc., 2004.
[5] Prasanna Kumari, "Women's Participation and Contribution to the Church," available from http://www.womenutc.com; accessed 9 July 2010.

Born-again at the age of 11, I knew from my early years that God has His hand on my life, and wanted me to do great exploits for Him. My parents instilled in me love for the Bible, but the theological perspective presented during my early years lay emphasis on the inferiority of women. Although the first chapter of Genesis described God as creating both the male and female in His image, suggesting equality between the two, at that time, most preachers focused on the second chapter of Genesis—that man was made first and that woman was made from a part of man to be his helper. Her inferiority was emphasized when they told us how Eve "brought sin into the world" by convincing Adam to eat from the forbidden tree. Because Eve sinned, God punished her by making her totally subservient to Adam's will. We were made to understand that Eve was transformed from Adam's helper into Adam's slave or property and this curse would be passed down to all the daughters of Eve; all women were deemed inferior at birth and inherited Eve's subservient role. Years later, another young pastor, Rev. Norman Prescott, prophetically uttered these words to me: "Mae, the Lord pulled back a curtain and allowed me to see a whole panorama of people and places around you. The Lord is sending you to the nations." But the negative messages echoed from childhood and hindered me from moving forward in my calling.

When Paul and Silas preached in Berea, a number of influential Greek women and men *received the word with all readiness of mind, and searched the Scriptures daily, whether those things were so.* This became my axiom and as soon as I was old enough, I began searching the Scriptures to understand: what the Bible teaches about the partnership of women and men in ministry. A thorough review of the key passages of Scripture pertinent to the equality and ministry of women is beyond the scope of this article. Suffice it to say that some churches by their strict and narrow interpretation of certain biblical texts, especially the writings of the Apostle Paul, are afraid to allow women to preach in public meetings for fear of being disobedient to the will of God. While it is imperative that we be obedient to the teachings of God's Word without compromise, we must always compare Scripture with Scripture to fully understand what the will of God is so that we worship God in spirit and in truth. In the light of the whole body of truth found in the New Testament teaching, I came to understand that God intended women and men to be in full partnership in marriage and ministry. Dr. Gilbert Bilezikian explains this in terms of the creation-fall-redemption hermeneutical model:[6]

1. Creation: God created human beings in His own image. Although they were different—male and female—there was no hint of inequality or hierarchy. The word "helper" does not connote inferiority. The specific context for God's provision of a "helper" to Adam is the affirmation that it was not good for him to be alone. He had been created to constitute community. But alone, he was not what he was made to be. Eve was created precisely to "help" him become the community of oneness that God had intended. "To wretch the word helper from this precise context, where it has the strength of a rescuer, and to invest it with connotations of domesticity or female subservience violates the intent of the biblical text."[7]

---

[6] Gilbert Bilezikian, *Beyond Sex Roles: What the Bible Says about a Woman's Place in Church and Family* (Grand Rapids: Baker Academic, 2006).
[7] Ibid, p. 22.

2. The Fall: Both Adam and Eve sinned. Although some traditions place blame on the Fall on Eve, the biblical text makes it clear Adam and Eve were together during the temptation; Adam had received instructions directly from God. As a result of sin, both were separated from God and from one another. Sexism, racism, genocide, rape, domestic violence, sex trafficking, child molestation, pornography and all other sins entered the world due to the Fall.

3. Redemption: Christ restored us back to God's original plan and purpose. Christ, our Redeemer, ascribed to women a measure of equality far beyond the expectations of the day, turning the patriarchal, hierarchical, and divisive society upside down. Through Christ—both male and female—have become one. "You are all sons of God through faith in Christ Jesus, for all of you who were baptized into Christ have clothed yourselves with Christ. There is neither Jew nor Greek, slave nor free, male nor female, for you are all one in Christ Jesus."[8]

The key principles of biblical equality are: that God freely calls believers to roles and ministries without regard to class, gender, or race. All have equal responsibility to use their gifts and obey their calling to the glory of God. Membership, ministry and mission are open to all in his kingdom, based on personal vocation, moral and personal qualifications and the gifts of the Holy Spirit.[9] That is biblical equality as God intended. But sins are not yet overcome and gradually the role of women reverted to the way it was before the time of the Fall.

---

[8] Galatians 3:26-28.

[9] Padgette, Alan, What is Biblical Equality? *Priscilla Papers,* Summer 2002:16:3, p. 22.

Nevertheless, we are redeemed in Christ and we can reclaim all that was lost in the Fall.

During my early years, few ministers even preached about biblical women. Many moving sermons were preached about biblical characters like Joseph, Moses, David, Samson, Daniel, Peter and Paul and they were portrayed as heroes of the faith. With the exception of Mary, the mother of Jesus, most sermons about women depicted "bad girls" like Lot's wife ("who looked back and turned to a pillar of salt"), Jezebel ("an evil and influential queen who corrupted Israel with idol worship and persecuted God's prophets"), Delilah ("an overt liar who made a mockery of Samson and caused his downfall"), Job's wife ("who told him to curse God and die"), Herodias ("who asked for the head of John the Baptist"), the "silly or gullible women" mentioned in 2 Timothy 3:1 – 7 and so on.

***

I was well into adulthood when I gained a wider perspective on biblical women. I do not ignore the "bad girls"; they had character flaws as all of us do. But I gained insight from studying other biblical women who impacted their nations in a positive way. Deborah was a prophet who judged Israel and led Barak to victory.[10] Huldah was a prophet who delivered God's message to King Josiah.[11] Esther was instrumental in saving her people from annihilation.[12] Rahab hid the two unnamed spies and saved the lives of her kinsmen.[13] Abigal acted wisely, and averted blood shed.[14] The Hebrew

---

[10] Judges 4:1-24.
[11] 2 Kings. 22:15-16.
[12] Esther 5-7.
[13] Judges 6:17.
[14] 1 Samuel 25:1-44.

midwives risked death to save lives.[15] The daughters of Zelophehad—Mahlah, Noah, Loglah, Milcah and Tirzah— challenged the inheritance laws, demanding that Moses give them the inheritance of their father. Their courageous stand changed the law for the entire nation of Israel.[16] Mary Magdalene, Joanna, Susanna, and many others traveled with Jesus and his male disciples at a time when the mixing of sexes was virtually unheard of. These women also "provided for the disciples out of their resources."[17] Women were the first to discover the empty tomb and they were sent first to share the good news of the risen Christ. Paul's first convert in Europe was a woman, Lydia, a wealthy merchant who provided for him, along with Pricilla, Aquila, and Philip's four daughters, who were prophetesses.

In spite of the predominance of male voices in the pulpit (and even in the biblical text itself) my faith was not shaken and I remained rooted and grounded in the Word. Dr. Renita Weems explains that,

> ...the Bible has been able to capture the imagination of African American women; it has been and continues to be able to do so because significant portions speak to the deepest aspirations of oppressed people for freedom, dignity, justice and vindication. Substantial portions of the Bible describe a world where the oppressed are liberated, the last become first, the humbled are exalted, the despised are preferred, those rejected are welcomed, the long-suffering are rewarded, the dispossessed are repossessed, and the arrogant are prostrated. And these are the passages, for oppressed

---

[15] Exodus 1:17-20.
[16] Numbers 36:1-13.
[17] Luke 8:1-3.

readers that stand at the center of the Biblical message and, thereby, serve as a vital norm for Biblical faith.[18]

The Lord confirmed my call into ministry in 1976. For twenty-seven years, I lived and worked in Africa serving in literacy ministry. I had opportunities to conduct training workshops in Angola, Benin, Burkina Faso, Burundi, Cameroon, Congo-Brazzaville, Côte d'Ivoire, Democratic Republic of Congo, Ethiopia, Ghana, Kenya, Liberia, Malawi, Madagascar, Mauritius, Mozambique, Nigeria, Rwanda, Sudan, Togo, Tanzania, Uganda, Zambia, Zimbabwe and other parts of the world. My passion has been to help churches start literacy programs so that people can read the Bible with understanding. Thousands of people came to know the Lord and churches were started in remote areas in Africa through the literacy ministry. Realizing the reality of the church and responding to God's call, I also took up the responsibility to help women and men learn biblical truths— go beyond human barriers and challenge systems of patriarchy that oppress and discriminate against people in the name of God.

Over the years, I have tried to educate people to see the problems of oppression, discrimination and gender inequalities and the need to redress them globally. Though it cannot be said that "all is well with women in the churches today," it can be said that the doors to ordination are open in several denominations, and structures of decision making bodies loosened to some extent; women are entering various ministries as pastors, seminary professors, prison chaplains, community

---

[18] Renita J Weems, "Reading *Her Way* through the Struggle: African American Women and the Bible," in *Stony the Road We Trod: African American Biblical Interpretation* ed. Cain Hope Felder (Minneapolis: Augsburg Fortress, 1991).

developers; in drug rehabilitation centers, in shelters for abused women, in rape crisis centers and so on.

Having relocated back to the United States, I am now serving on the Adjunct Faculty at Beulah Heights University, teaching courses in missions, cross-cultural communication, writing and theology. My challenge is to educate this younger generation which has seen scandal affect every institution from the stock market to the Presidency and the Church. During their childhood, the divorce rate tripled. Some of them are un-parented and un-churched. Just as some of them were about to hit the workforce, the economy began to steadily decline. Competition for jobs was tight especially for minorities; this has persisted to the present time. The American Dream had changed. For the first time in history, this generation is being told that they will not be able to replicate the lifestyles of their parents' generation. Whereas my generation viewed the future with optimism and expectancy, this generation finds the future disheartening and question if they even have a future. Typically, they have little trust in hierarchies and they offer little or no loyalty to institutions. This generation has grown up in an era of technology with cable television, cell phones, laptop computers, ipods, and video games, which serve to drive their expectation of immediacy. They have been described as the best educated generation—and they know it! However, the quality of the education is not always reflected in their interest in reading books and writing papers. They often use phonetic spelling to speed the process of written communication.[19]

To reach this generation, I need to be transparent—keeping it real is important to them. I need to mentor, coach, teach, preach, and even provoke them to challenge gender

---

[19] (No Author given), "Managing a Multigenerational Workforce, The Diversity Manager's Toolkit," Cook Ross, Inc, 2004.

inequality, to counteract man-made theologies that are loud, strong but wrong! In the context of the 21st century, my task to empower my students is four-fold:

- To break barriers and enter into church structures which are male-dominated, misogynist, and patriarchal.[20]
- To confront issues of materialism and secularism within the Church, recover biblical values, and reclaim the ministries of the church to holy living.
- To confront evils in the larger culture such as sexism, racism, genocide, rape, domestic violence, human trafficking and so on.
- To write their stories so that those coming behind them will benefit from their experiences in life and ministry

These tasks are not easy. But when God calls us, He empowers us with the Holy Spirit and strengthens us to be God's voice to the church and to the world.

---

[20] Kumari, op.cit.

Silent No More: A Global Perspective
By Anyango E. Reggy, Ph.D.

Throughout the world, women are subjected to violence, discrimination, and neglect simply because they are women. This is true in the developing world as much as in the economically advanced countries. Women have less access to education, and healthcare; they remain severely under-represented in politics, and they make less money than men for the same jobs. Case in point, last year there were more women in the United States who received Ph.D. degrees than ever before, and yet on average, female college professors make about $10,000 less than their male colleagues.[21]

Beyond the economic discrimination, physical violence is another issue that a majority of women are confronted with on a daily basis. The United Nations Development Fund for Women (UNIFEM) reports that "Violence against women and girls is one of the most widespread violations of human rights."[22] UNIFEM further notes that six out of every ten women worldwide are subjected to physical and/or sexual violence in their lifetime.[23]

An eye-opening article by New York Times columnist Bob Herbert titled "Punished for Being Female" recounts the

---

[21] Daniel de Vise, *More Women Than Men Got PhDs Last Year*, available from http://www.washingtonpost.com; accessed 14 September 2010.
[22] UNIFEM, *Violence Against Women*, available from http://www.unifem.org; accessed on 14 September 2010.
[23] Ibid.

countless ways in which women have been emotionally and physically damaged by cultural practices and traditions—as well as laws, and policies—that severely disadvantage them. Herbert writes of, "Bride burnings, honor killings, female infanticide, sex trafficking, mass rape as a weapon of war and many other hideous forms of violence against women..." [24] Herbert further reports that the most common and severe forms of abuse against women in Australia, Canada, Israel, and the United States are committed by husbands and boyfriends. A study conducted in the U.S. found homicide to be "the second leading cause of death for girls 15 to 18."[25] Of these, at least seventy-eight per cent were slain "by an acquaintance or intimate partner." [26]

Many scholars[27] have observed that economic, psychological, and physical violence meted out against women stem from the structural or patriarchal global arrangements, which relegate women to second-class citizenship status in every country in the world. Moreover, despite the fact that women throughout history have made tremendous contributions to the growth and development of their nations, their efforts have gone largely unrecognized.

However, because of the tireless efforts by an array of advocates such as women's organizations, civil society groups, and that of institutions like the United Nations, several of these male dominated structures have been a target for positive

---

[24] Bob Herbert, *Punished for Being Female*, available from http://select.nytimes.com; accessed 30 September 2010.
[25] Ibid.
[26] Ibid.
[27] In *The Masculine Self* (New York: Sloan Publishing, 2007), Christopher Kilmartin clearly outlines the negative impact of patriarchy on both men and women.

destruction. Similarly, governments have also recently joined in the struggle for the empowerment of women with policies directly meant to remedy this problem. For instance, the government of Rwanda introduced a quota system to ensure that women are fairly represented in politics. Today, with fifty-six percent[28] women in parliament, Rwanda has the highest number of elected female officials in the world.

While the Church should be playing a leading role in the struggle for gender equality as part of its mission, its silence on these issues has been deafening. Not only has the Church failed to serve as a refuge for women, it has contributed to the cultural silencing of women.

It is important to note that there are a number of Christian leaders who have publicly condemned this global misogyny. For instance, in 2002, the United Conference of Catholic Bishops asserted, "we state as clearly and strongly as we can that violence against women, inside or outside the home, is *never* justified. Violence in any form '—physical, sexual, psychological, or verbal'—is sinful..." The statement goes on to say, "We have called for a moral revolution to replace a culture of violence."[29]

In general, however, the Church has failed to denounce the mistreatment of women. It has, instead, exacerbated the gender inequalities that are prevalent in the society at large. Christian author Ruth Haley Barton articulates it this way, "Rather than living out God's ideal of women and men in

---

[28] Sarah Boseley, *Rwanda: A Revolution in Rights for Women*, available from http://www.guardian.co.uk.; accessed 3 October 2010.

[29] United States Conference of Catholic Bishops, *When I Call for Help: A Pastoral Response to Domestic Violence Against Women,* available http://www.usccb.org/laity/help.shtml; accessed 2 October 2010.

equally partnership in such a way that our presence in society begins to transform it, we have created elaborate systems, rules, and structures that segregate and limit us."[30] Similarly, in their reflections on gender and religion, Rev. Dr. Marie M. Fortune and Rabbi Cindy G. Enger maintain that, "Religious institutions have explicitly or implicitly shaped the context of values which have tolerated violence against women." [31]

Sadly, one of the prevailing male chauvinistic ideologies is the notion that women are inferior to men. Rejecting this notion, former U.S. President Jimmy Carter argues, "The truth is that male religious leaders have had—and still have—an option to interpret holy teachings either to exalt or subjugate women. They have, for their own selfish ends, overwhelmingly chosen the latter."[32]

Furthermore, while women make up a large percentage of the membership of churches, and diligently contribute their time, money, and service to their local churches, many women continue to be hindered from participating fully and equally in the Church.[33] Barton notes, "For many religious women, their deepest wounds have been inflicted by a church that has silenced them and excluded them from full part in the life of the church." [34]

---

[30] Ruth Haley Barton, "Created for Life Together," in *Equal To The Task: Men and Women in Partnership* (Downers Grove: InterVarsity Press, 1998), 19.

[31] Rev. Dr. Marie Fortune and Rabbi Cindy G. Enger, *Violence Against Women and the Role of Religion,* available http://new.vawnet.org/category/Main_Doc.php?docid=411; accessed 7 July 7 2010.

[32] Jimmy Carter, *The Words of God Do Not Justify Cruelty To Women,* available from http://www.guardian.co.uk; accessed 18 July 2010.

[33] Ibid.

[34] Barton, op.cit., 19.

This author maintains that as a whole, men have benefited from a system that continues to privilege them over women. Men, therefore, preachers and congregates alike, have a responsibility to speak out against the marginalization and discrimination of women in the Church and within society as a whole. Likewise, women must boldly challenge patriarchy which severely disadvantages them wherever they reside. They must reclaim their rightful place in the kingdom of God. Author Lee Grady observes, "Jesus modeled a revolutionary new paradigm of empowerment by affirming women as co-heirs of God's grace."[35] Women of God can be silent no more!

[35] Lee Grady quoted in Sue Bohlin, Probe Ministries 5 *Lies the Church Tells Women*, available from
http://www.leaderu.com/orgs/probe/docs/5lies.html; accessed 5 October 2010.

PART 2

It's Time to Tell Our Stories

"When I think about the title of this book, Silent No More, it brings this big ole grin to my face, but it also brings big ole tears to my eyes. It is probably because I have these vivid childhood memories embedded in my brain of always being told to shut up, and sit down. No one really wanted to listen to me, no one really cared that I had a voice. But I thank God everyday that I am silent no more. I have been given the opportunity to speak out and speak up. No one tells me to shut up anymore. Things sure have a way of turning around in your life."

Beverly Ponder
Speaking Out of Experience

Understanding My Path
By Patricia Jones

"I can do all things through Christ which strengtheneth me."[36]

As I stood looking down the path that was before me, I found myself alone. Never before had I felt such a feeling. My past lay behind me and my future before me. I do not know how long I stood there before it hit me, I was at a crossroad. Not knowing what was in front of me but not wanting to revisit what was behind me, I fell on my knees and buried my face in my hands. My insides cried out louder than any sound I had ever made with my mouth. When the sound stopped, there was an echo resonating back to me, telling my mind that I wanted to be saved, that I needed to be saved.

I awoke to the sounds of cars going by. I realized I had been dreaming. I wanted so badly to go back to sleep, to escape from the empty ache in my soul that longed for the laughter of children; my children. How had I ended up at this point? Where had I gone wrong? My mind started to replay the tape that had been played for what seemed like an eternity. When would it end? How would it end? LORD, please let it be a happy ending!

I was good. I treated people right. Why had my childhood desires turned into a nightmare?

I finally pulled myself out of bed and let in a little sunlight. Not as much as I was used to, but enough to see the

---

[36] Philippians 4:13

mess my house had become. Without the love and laughter of my children, it was no longer a home.

I made my way to the bathroom, not pausing to look in the mirror, and then to the kitchen. Opening the refrigerator, I was reminded that once again I had spent everything... everything, on drugs. The only time the desire to do right hit me like this was after a binge on drugs and alcohol. It was these occurrences that got my children taken from me, my family to give up on me, and my friends long gone.

Satan appeared to have the upper hand, but I would never claim it. I called on God more than I ever had but it seemed my plight was mine to deal with because nothing seemed to change.

As usual, the anger started to cover the pain and I began to indulge in self-pity. Why try? Why keep praying? Why keep going through this? GOD, why have you forsaken me? What am I to do?

It did not take long to decide what I was going to do. I found something to put on and I went back to the streets, the only place I was not alone...physically.

That was many years ago.

The day God came to get me would appear to many to be the worst day of my life, but to me it was the best. There was no fairy tale ending to my dysfunction. I had to go through life changing experiences for restoration and right standing with God, but He led me all the way.

There were days that standing still was all I could do, but going backwards was never an option. I learned what faith really felt like, and what blessings really looked like. For most of my life I had given only lip service to the word faith, but life had taught me a valuable lesson. It requires more than lip service to work.

I was ready to have God do what was needed to be done for my life to change. I stood steadfast and faced myself and started on the path to my salvation.

God had called me to teach His word years before my path took on its downward spiral, and now it was time to accept my call.

I questioned my ability to do the work I had been called to do because of my past, but I was reminded by God that my past paved the way for what has become my future.

My life was restored, my children came home, my family showed support, and my real friends, never left.

I went to work and I worked hard and moved forward in life at a pace that surprised everyone including me. I knew God had all power but never before had I personally been on the receiving end the way I was now.

I returned to school and acquired my degree and started to share so generously what God had so generously given to me.

Speaking Out of Experience
By Beverly Ponder

Writing this chapter made me think of the words of a song that I love, called "Untold Story." Each time I hear the song, these words touch my heart; *"If I told you my untold story would you stay, or just walk away? You don't know the price I paid for this anointing on my life."* Now I can say that there is an anointing on my life, but it was not always there. God has brought me from a mighty long way. If it had not been for God on my side, I would probably be dead. I pray that this chapter will help some woman or man, who may be struggling in their life and ministry. My prayer is that comfort, encouragement, ability, and the potential to fly will be found within these pages.

***

My mother gave birth to me at age nineteen while my father was only twenty-two years old. Although they were married, it did not make them a family. It was just a marriage so that I could have my father's last name. Having a child out of wedlock carried a stigma in those days. I was raised by my grandparents in a Christian home, along with two sisters, one older and one younger than me. We went to church seven days a week, rain or snow, hot or cold. On Saturdays we prepared for Sunday services—mentally, spiritually, and physically. We were in church all day on Sunday, from morning until six o'clock in the evening. Our Sunday evenings were spent watching the, "old gospel channel." There was only one television and one channel. So all of us watched the same program. Our home was always full of people who loved, laughed, cried, prayed, and played. My grandparents did not allow any foolishness (as my grandfather called it) to go on in the home, so there was seldom any yelling or arguing heard in our home. I guess I can say I had a happy childhood.

When I was around eight years old, I became very sick. I was taken to Beth Israel Hospital in Newark, New Jersey, where I was diagnosed as having a touch of polio. This sickness made me weak and unable to stand for about two weeks, but I recovered, or I thought I had. In July of the next year, I was diagnosed with rheumatic fever. This was the turning point in my life. Having visited my mother for the weekend, I remember being carried back to my grandmother's house and being laid on the sofa downstairs where the pot belly stove warmed the room. I remember hearing the crackling of the wood and feeling so safe and warm knowing that my grandmother was going to help me walk again. I had overheard the doctors telling my mother in whispered tones that I would never walk again or if I did, it would be with a limp. But something happened on that evening. Happenings that would set in motion events in my life—both good and bad—as I journeyed toward God.

My grandmother who was completely blind began to pray over me. Her praying was not unusual because this is what Grandma did all the time. But this time she prayed with her hands cupped over my face and she began to repeat the same words over and over, "From this time forward, your eyes will be only on Jesus. You shall walk into your destiny." I do not know how many times Grandma said that, but is seemed like a lot. I had no idea that she was uttering prophesy over my life because I was an eight year old child who had just become partially paralyzed. I am grateful to God that I received complete healing. But not long after that my grandmother died, and this began a dark time in my life. *"If I told you my untold story would you stay, or just walk away?"*

After my grandmother's death, my sisters and I went to live with our mother. By this time, she had given birth to yet another daughter. It was a hard life because my mother was an alcoholic, and I became the mother to my two younger sisters while I was still a child myself. Most times I was okay with it, but other times I wanted so badly to just be a child. My daddy had moved on with his life, marrying again, and by now even my step-father had moved on because of my mother's heavy drinking. *"If I told you my untold story would you stay, or just walk away?"*

I have always loved going to church; it was an outlet for me, and I felt so at home whenever I was there. But the church also became my hurting ground. When I was around twelve years old, I was molested by a deacon in the church. After that ordeal, I became broken, embarrassed, and bruised. I always believed that Jesus loved me, but after this happened, I felt Jesus was angry with me and did not love me anymore. From then on it seemed as if there was a neon sign on my forehead that caused men to abuse me sexually such as my mother's drinking partners. When I would tell her about it, she ignored me or called me negative names always making reference to my being dark-skinned. My mother was light skinned— "high-yella" as people used to say. *"If I told you my untold story would you stay, or just walk away?"*

By the time I turned fourteen, my mother had had a mental breakdown, and I was left to raise my two younger sisters alone. My grandfather put us up in an apartment and became our overseer. During those times, it was not proper for young women who had started their menstruation to live in a home alone with a man. So we had to live separate from him. My grandfather was my "god" in a sense. There was no problem he could not solve; but he would never be able to solve my problems of shame, depression, or anger. No, only the true and living God could do that. After some years, I mended physically, but my mind was troubled. I feared that I too, as my mother, would lose my mind. What plans had God for me to allow this horror to happen to me? I still cannot answer that. I spent most of my years hiding. I was always hiding from people, hiding from hurt and pain, hiding from myself, hiding, hiding, and hiding. I had a mask for every event, while I tried to find a smile behind my tears. *"If I told you my untold story would you stay, or just walk away?"*

At eighteen I had my first son, and now I had not only him to care for, but my two sisters, and by now, one of my sisters had her own baby. Yet I still remained as true to God as I could remember how. At age nineteen I married my son's father and had my second son. No one told me the horror I would face for the years to come. I was wedded to an abusive man who thought beating, kicking, choking, and dragging me around was an act of love. I prayed as the Bible said I should, but God did not answer. I cried out to God, but it was as if God had gone deaf. The Baptist Church in which I belonged said that I could not leave my spouse because it would not be the Christian thing to do. Five sons were born in this marriage and raising them kept me sane. I loved my sons so much and I did not want them to be looked down on as children from a broken home. So for twenty-one years I remained in the marriage as my sons and I suffered abuse. Yet, I continued to hold on to the God of the Scriptures believing that one day He would rescue us from this place of despair.

On my thirty-second birthday, I made a final decision to leave my marriage, but as soon as I left, it seemed as if the devil was standing on the other side of the door waiting for me. I always believed that I was saved, but I was about to find out how just how lost I really was. I did things I would never have thought I would do. I became like my mother, although addicted to a different drug of choice. I was trying so hard to escape the abuse I had endured for twenty-one years, but I could find no way out. I was trapped inside of myself, and I really needed God to deliver me, but at the same time I was convinced that God had failed me. Maybe I had resolved myself to a lifestyle of sin because I had gotten tired of fighting, and feeling that God had abandoned me. *"If I told you my untold story would you stay, or just walk away?"*

My sons' father decided to walk completely out of their lives leaving me to raise them alone. It was both hard and easy at the same time. It was hard, because my desire was to raise my sons in a two-parent household where they could learn to become men of honor, but easy because the abuse had stopped. I met and married my second spouse in 1985. He was wonderful to me and my five sons. My spouse, as well as my sons loved me unconditionally, but I remained bound to my past and continued walking in hurt, anger and disguises. Although I pretended I was happy, I had only found another hiding place.

In 1993, God called me into the ministry to preach and teach His Word, but I could not accept His call. So I did not respond. I had allowed my mind to be trapped in a world of sin and shame. A trap had been set for me by the enemy, and I was falling deeper into it every day. I felt that God could not have really called me because I was too rotten, and stinking with sin to be used by such a holy God. This God who expected people to live clean and holy lives surely was in error calling on me. Shame had become my hiding place, and I was not able to unveil my pain to a world that had caused it. Somewhere along life's path, I had lost the fervency I had for God. There was something—like a wall—that kept me from allowing God to get too close. Maybe all the years of horrible pain had hardened my heart. I had not dealt with the molestation and abuse I had suffered and I blamed God for allowing it to happen. I had buried it so deep that it did not resurface until I was fifty years old. I still went to church, but it was more out of tradition than out of love for God. I kept going probably so that my children would continue going. I sung in the choir, served on the usher board, taught Sunday school, and went to weekly prayer meeting. I did everything a good ole Christian would do, but deep down inside I was hurting and angry. Yes, I was hurting, but there was always something on the inside of me that made me hunger for God's love. I just did not know that I was already getting a daily dose of it. I could not see or hear beyond the pain that drove me. I spent the next years running from the call placed on my life. I tell you that I ran hard and fast, but it would not let me go. *"If I told you my untold story would you stay, or just walk away?"*

My call to preach came again on September 13, 1999. I remember that date well because I had just buried my second spouse, and I was angry with God again. I remember as I stood next to the stove preparing a cup of tea, I heard the voice of God. Yes, I still knew His voice. Remember what the Word says, "My sheep hear my voice, and I know them, and they follow me."[37] It was not something I felt in my heart, but it was actually an audible voice. But the anger I felt toward God had hardened me. My mother had died and as strange as it might sound, I did not grieve her passing, but when my second spouse died, I completely fell apart. Now I had no one else left to hide behind. The times in my grandparent's living room were far from my thoughts and I was angry and feeling like I had

---

[37]John 10:27.

nothing to live for. So my response to God was, "I am not hearing or listening to you anymore!" I really said that to God. The pain I allowed to grow within me for so long would not allow me to surrender to the call from God. *"Now will you stay if I told you my story or will you still walk away?"*

There is an old cliché that says, "There is always light at the end of the tunnel". In this instance, that cliché' became reality. 1999 was not just a year of loss. It also became the year my life changed drastically—it became the year of my rebirth. What was once dead came back to life! I finally accepted my call and it began an earth shattering deliverance in my life. The Scripture in Isaiah 6:1 says: *"In the year that King Uzziah died, I saw the Lord sitting on a throne, high and lifted up, and the train of His robe filled the temple."*[38] Like Isaiah, I began to realize that the very thing that had been keeping me back had just been removed. My King Uzziah was my spouse. For so long he was my co-dependent, my blind spot. He supplied what I needed for that time, but it was only temporal, and I was only happy as long as I was getting what I thought I needed. Although I loved him very much, once he was removed, I had no other choice but to see God. My walls came crashing down around me and there I stood naked before God for the entire world to see. It was now time for me to face me.

Did I forget to tell you that I did not love me? I had not loved me since that time the deacon molested me. Did I forget to tell you when my mother's friends raped me, they killed me inside—little by little? I had become dead to my own feelings. But now it was time to face my anger, pain, and shame. I had no one to hide behind, no one to use as cover. I needed God to lead and direct me. I needed to be reintroduced to that fearfully and

---

[38] Isaiah 6:1.

wonderfully made person God had created. I was a person who had been lost within herself for far too long. I had no idea how I was suppose to love me when within me there was still a hurting little girl. When was she going to heal? What was I suppose to say to her? How was I going to tell her that I was sorry that no one helped, and that although they left her sitting in a dark place for so long, I really did love her? I had no words for her, but I knew with God's help I would find them.

The little girl within me finally started to heal, but it took a long time before she became well enough to tell her story. See, the one thing that I had forgotten to do when I was hurting was to acknowledge my pain. People would tell me that I was strong and that I did not let anything bother me. If they had only known that I was spit-fire mad and hurting almost all of the time. I was so busy trying to be everything for everyone that I had forgotten how to be real. But I am telling you, it is all right to scream and holler if it is going to keep you from losing your mind. It is all right to express yourself when you are hurting because it will keep you out of bondage. I was so busy faking it, I got locked up in my own hell. Now, I can truthfully say that I am walking in the freedom that God has delivered me to. I am no longer angry, no longer hostile, and no longer ashamed. I am a new creature and old things have passed away. I am a woman on a mission with a ministry.

Today I am an ordained minister. I received my Associates in Biblical Education, Bachelors in Biblical Education, and Masters in Biblical Studies from Beulah Heights University where I am presently seeking my Masters in Divinity. My near future educational plan is to receive my Doctorate of Ministry and maybe go on to earn a Ph.D. God has gifted me in the area of loving women through deliverance. I have a great love and respect for women of all races, creeds, and colors. The reason I can love these women the way I do is because I am one of them.

Through my sorrows and through my tears, I know God as my deliverer. I am more than sure that God is a way maker. I know without a doubt that God is a rescuer. When I think about my past, it no longer brings tears to my eyes, but praises to my lips. You see, God has been more than good to me. God healed me so that I was able to walk again both physically as well as spiritually. I was given the gift to lead, the compassion to love, and the skills to mentor. All of those gifts given to me by God were used as I raised my sisters who are now mothers and grandmothers. I have been able to forgive those men who saw no shame in what they did. I forgave my father for leaving me, and my mother for not loving me enough to care. I have even forgiven that spouse who loved with his fist. I am free from the bondage of sin through the death, burial, and resurrection of Jesus Christ. I am more than a conqueror and I overcame my past. I love the way David says in the Psalm 139:1-4, 14:

> O LORD, you have examined my heart and know everything about me. You know when I sit down or stand up. You know my every thought when far away. You chart the path ahead of me and tell me where to stop and rest. Every moment you know where I am. You know what I am going to say even before I say it, LORD. Thank you for making me so wonderfully complex! Your workmanship is marvelous and how well I know it.

Out of all of my past pain and sorrow, hurts and despair, City of Rest Transitional Home for Women Phase I, will soon be birthed. This will house, nurture, teach, love, and direct women who found themselves in the penal system, or addicted to drugs, or stuck in a past similar to mine. Phase II will reconnect them back to their children. I no longer have to scratch and fight to fit into this calling on my life. I am more than sure of my calling and my purpose. All I have to do is just follow God's guidance.

God has also blessed me to finally have a husband. If you noticed, I have never used this word—husband—before. That is because this man—who I am proud to call my husband— is definitely a husband in every sense of the word. We are equally yoked in the things of God, and our marriage is a ministry unto God. My husband supports me totally in the things of God while he helps me to remain free from the things of my past. What a man—what a mighty good man!

Can I, and will I continue to speak out of my experience? Every day of my life! I will share the miracles God has done for me, so you will know that it can be done for you too. The love of God has kept my heart and my mind in perfect peace. I am compelled by the love of God to share my story with those who find themselves in the gutters of despair as I was. I will no longer remain silent about circumstances that have caused my anointing to be so great. My past is no longer a place of despair and bondage for me. It has become a place where I re-visit to help others, but knowing that I have left it behind forever. *"Now if I told you my untold story, will you stay, or will you walk away? You still don't know the price I paid for this anointing on my life."* But, it really does not matter; just know this, "I have seen the Lord sitting on a throne, high and lifted up, and His train will always fill my temple!"

Cry into your deliverance; Cry into your freedom; Cry into the voice God established within you in his original design; Cry for all those no one cried for; cry for the abandoned, for the molested, for the abused; for the lonely; for the motherless; for the fatherless; for the dead souls afraid to choose life; for the generations yet unborn; for the nations! I guess what I am really asking you THIS DAY is will you walk with me in the purpose now established as God has ordained and decide this day to choose life? In this choosing will you commit to be the voice of freedom in God? Will you rise up and determine this day to be SILENT NO MORE? Who will cry for the little boys/girls; for the men/women? We will; won't you join us and cry for them too, in the image of our father, Jesus Christ? He is waiting! And so are they! What will you do this day? I cried today and set you free. Now it is your turn. Will you take this vow to be SILENT NO MORE? Who will cry for the little boys/girls; for the men/women? You and I will cry together.[39]

---

[39] Annette L. Bettis, *Her Dance Defines Life*. Bettis is an up and coming writer.

Finding Strength in Adversity
By Rebecca Manning

I was born in Mississippi and grew up in a small town in California. We were a large family and considered poor by most standards. My mother worked in the fields picking fruit and later went to work in a cannery. My father worked in a warehouse. Both my parents made very little money. During this time there was no such thing as food stamps. Needy families stood in line and received a box of commodities. The box contained cheese, butter, oatmeal, and canned meat. It helped feed our family throughout the month.

The neighbors talked badly about us. I was hurt when I overheard the neighbors saying, "Those kids will never amount to anything. There are just too many of them." As children, we used to say, "Sticks and stones may break your bones, but words can never hurt you." How wrong this saying was. I would have rather been hit with a stick or a stone because that pain would have faded away, but the neighbors' words remained embedded in my mind. At the same time, these same words became the catalysts that drove me to do better, live better, and help those in my family and others do the same.

We were eleven children in the family, seven boys and four girls. I have five older siblings and five younger siblings. I am the middle child. When the midwife delivered me at home in Mississippi, she told my mother that I would never survive because I only weighed three pounds. Well, if the devil wanted to stop me, he had his chance then.

Like most other families, we had our share of problems. My father drank a lot. He drank up a good portion of the little money he made or spent it on other women. Whenever he came home drunk, I knew what was about to happen—someone was going to get a whipping. He only whipped my brothers when he got drunk. He whipped them over dumb stuff like closing the door too hard or he would make up an excuse to whip one of them. On those nights, I would burst through the back screen door without unhooking the one hook that kept it shut and run as fast as I could to get to the edge of the field behind our house. I could not bear to hear my brothers cry when my father whipped them. After it was all over, I wanted to comfort them, but I could not until our father fell off to sleep. Terrified I would get caught, I crawled on my hands and knees into the one room shared by my brothers, to give comfort to the one who got a whipping that day. "It's okay," I would say, "someday you will be all grown up, and there will be no more whippings." To see them hurt made me very sad. I wished a million times that I could have taken them far, far away from my father.

Growing up I knew the church as the place that gave us a Thanksgiving and Christmas food basket. There was also a neighbor lady, Ms. Ward, who talked my mother into letting us go to Sunday school. At Second Baptist church, I began to learn about the Lord. It was at this small Baptist church where I learned the Bible stories and that Jesus loved me. It was hard to believe because I had a different concept of a father. My father was an angry and abusive man. I never felt he loved or wanted me or my brothers and sisters. He had a slave master mentality. Children were only good for working and waiting on him hand and foot. When my mother cooked, he always made himself a plate of food to eat then and set aside another plate of food to eat later. Whatever was left was divided among eleven children

44

and my mother. Often, I would not eat so that my mother would have something to eat.

I never heard my father say he loved me, and I do not believe he told any of my brothers or sisters that he loved them. Not in defense of his actions, but to make some sense of them, I think part of my father's anger and alcoholism was because he could neither read nor write; he could only sign his name. He served in the Navy as a cook and a boxer. I used to see my mother, who had only a fourth grade education, sitting on the bed reading the mail to him as best she could. I thought to myself that he was too lazy to read the mail himself, so he made my mother read it to him. I soon found out the truth. I believe I was in the sixth grade when I started reading the mail. This was something I did until my mother went on to be with the Lord. She saved all the mail until I came to read it, because she trusted no one else. I remember, while working in the Virgin Islands, I called her, and she tried to read mail to me to get an understanding of what it contained. I thought I had talked her into letting someone else read the mail, but when I arrived home from the island, she had a stack of mail for me to read.

My sister Marie was the first person in our family to live a Christian life. She shared the Bible with me and taught me what she knew. She was sweet and angelic. Living in Mississippi, she was not given the care she needed. She had rheumatic fever and suffered serious damage to her heart. So she needed heart surgery. It sounded so simple. She would go into the hospital, the doctors would fix the problem, and she would come home and live a normal life. The day she left for the hospital, I was very sad and worried about her. She gave me her teddy bear and told me to take care of it until she came home. That day my class had gone on a field trip to the bowling alley. I remember someone coming to get me but on the long drive home no one told me what had happened. My mind was racing. I did not know what to think, but I prayed. When I got home I was told that Marie had died. I wanted to know why. She was young, living a holy life and she died. I wanted my sister back.

Being a Christian did not mean that I would not suffer pain or heartache. Many times in the midst of anger, sadness, or fear, I cried out to the Lord for an answer. I felt it was unfair that my sister was gone. I needed an answer. After crying myself to sleep, for what seemed like an eternity, one night my sister appeared to me in a dream. She was wearing a beautiful white dress—the dress she was buried in. In the dream she comforted me. She let me know that she was with the Lord and we would be together again someday and that the Lord would be with me always. *"The eyes of the Lord are on the righteous and His ears are attentive to their cry.... The righteous cry out, and the Lord hears them... The Lord is close to the broken hearted and saves those who are crushed in spirit."*[40]

The next morning, I felt refreshed and the sadness I felt was gone. I cried no more. I went to church with two of my friends and we agreed that we would join. When the altar call was made, I went forward and they did not. One of them ended up in prison and the other suffers from mental illness brought on by drug abuse. Had it not been for the Lord on my side, where would I be? At that time, I did not know the difference between joining the church and giving my heart to the Lord. No one talked to me about salvation. "The doors of the church are open," the pastor said, and I came forward to join the church.

---

[40] Psalm 34:15, 17-18.

The next few years, I felt as if I was wandering through life. There was so much I just did not understand. The relationship I had with my father made it hard for me to see the heavenly Father as a kind, gentle loving God. I only knew this man that did not love us. I wanted desperately to have a loving relationship with my father. I wanted to please him so I tried to be a good daughter. I wanted him to respond to me the way other fathers responded to their children, yet I was afraid of him. I constantly worried about my mother and my brothers with him in the house. Little did I know that a storm was brewing that was going to change my life and close the door on my childhood forever.

One evening, my father said he was taking me to get ice cream. I was so happy and excited that he wanted to take me and no one else could go. We drove and drove until I finally asked where we were going. He said he had to make a stop someplace. Soon we were in an isolated area of town. He pulled the car over and told me to pull my pants down. I asked him why and he took a condom out of his pocket and placed it on his fingers. I was afraid and struggled not to cry. I summoned all the courage I had and told him, "No!" My father said he wanted me to experience this act with him so that I would not get involved with other boys. Terrified, I told him that *I wanted to go home and I was not going to pull my pants down, that he would have to kill me to get my pants off!* I began screaming, "Take me home!" With that, he started the car and drove, what seemed like days, until we finally arrived home. My heart was forever broken. I never related to him as a little girl and would never relate to him as an adult woman. This was the last time I was ever in a car or any place alone with my father.

After the incident with my father, I grew to hate him. My father began to tell my mother that he suspected that I might be on drugs. I thought this is how he would explain himself if I ever told her. He would say I lied and I was on drugs but this incident also worked in my favor. When my father was arguing with my mother, I could walk into the room and glare at him and he would stop. I gave him a look that said *I am going to expose you for the rotten man that you are.* Even then, I worried about having children of my own and not being able to leave them with my mother for fear that my father would harm them. I did not tell anyone because I thought I would be removed from my home and put in another home. I have trusted this secret with no one except the readers of this story. I was confused and hurt and blamed myself. I could have been a better daughter, I thought, and moved from anger to hurt to shame. Women must know that when molestation occurs between an adult and a child, the child bears no fault. The adult is in control and the child is powerless against them. There is nothing children can do to entice, compel or cause an adult to commit a sexual act against them. The adult fully understands they are involving a child and knows right from wrong. Every woman who has been molested as a child must know that it is not her fault. I truly believe the Lord sent an angel that night on the side of the road. When I spoke those words to my father it sounded like the roar of a mighty lion and he drove me home.

My father became ill and it was believed his illness was related to a back injury he suffered. We later learned that my father had been stricken with cancer. When I learned the news—as awful as it sounds—I felt relieved that he possibly would not live to be near my children. But I also became angry. I did not want him to die before he apologized to me. With each day that passed, I hoped he would tell me he was sorry and had made a terrible mistake. I wanted something more than the memory of that evening. Yet, nothing was to come. I became angry with God. I had a terrible father and He took my sweet sister. I attended church and worked in the church but I was not serving the Lord. I attended Sunday school and even sang in the choir but had no real relationship with God.

By the time my father's cancerous condition reached a terminal stage, I was married and carrying my first child. The telephone rang late one night and my husband answered the call. When he came to bed, I asked who had called and he said it was a wrong number. The next morning after getting a full night's rest, my husband told me my father died. My father died and I never got that apology I hoped for. I went to view my father's body and observed lines on the side of his eyes. It was as if he had been hit by an intense wave of pain that caused him to close his eyes tightly and the pain was so intense that the lines remained. As I looked at him, I was still angry with some level of satisfaction that he had experienced pain. *"Why are you downcast, O my soul? Why so disturbed within me? Put your hope in God, for I will yet praise Him, my Savior and my God."* [41]

Unfortunately, I married a man much like my father. He ran around with other women, drank too much, and was physically and verbally abusive to me. I lived in fear in my own home. He controlled where I went, how long I stayed there, and when I could come home. He picked me up from work and some days, he would be out with his friends and leave me waiting two hours. If I accepted a ride from anyone, he would beat me, so I waited until he came. If we were out, I did not dare look around because he would accuse me of looking at other men. He would go out and stay out all night and the only place I could go was to work, home, and to my mother's house. He would start fights in public and I would be terrified to go home

---

[41] Psalm 42:11.

with him. I somehow felt I deserved this type of treatment because I had such a terrible father.

While in high school, I was not allowed to date, so I dated my then boyfriend, behind my parents' back. After I graduated from high school I introduced him to my father. He bought my father a bottle of Seagram 7, his favorite alcoholic beverage, and my father thought he walked on water. The abuse began soon after I met him and continued throughout our marriage. When I walked down the aisle on our wedding day, I knew then that I should not marry him. I wanted to run from the church, but I did not know how to get out of it. Women, understand that it does not matter if the church is decorated and the guests have all arrived, if you know the relationship is wrong, *do not* go through with it. Deep down I prayed he would change but he did not. Do not marry a man and expect that you will change him.

I bore two beautiful children and they were the source of my happiness. I devoted myself to them and stayed out of my husband's way as much as I could. I lived in a beautiful home, drove a nice car, and had a lot of things because he was a good provider. But none of these things shielded me from his abuse. I wanted a better life for me and my children, but I felt it was hopeless. I lived in fear and thought one day he would kill me.

After my father died, I helped my mother raise my five brothers. For the most part, they did well considering they had no father. Even with him in the home, he was never a father to us. I love my brothers. Now, let me tell you about my brother Matthew.

Matthew and I would sit and talk for hours. He was a kind, gentle person. He was also very smart. He graduated from high school and was excited about joining the U.S. Army, but army life was mean and cruel and it changed him. When he was discharged from the military, he drank a lot and his behavior became more erratic. He was afraid his food was being contaminated by family members, so he washed his food, then cooked it, then washed it again. He worked washing windows and began accusing my mother of trying to steal his business. I was in constant prayer for him. We tried to get him help but needed his consent. He could not give his consent because he did not realize he was sick. So he received no help and his condition only worsened.

One night he told my mother he was moving into his own place. The next morning, when she awakened, he was gone. We searched unsuccessfully for two years. We got a lead that he had gotten a traffic ticket in Los Angeles and inquired about his address. The address we were given turned out to be a vacant lot. Over the years I had many dreams of him and each time he was wearing an army uniform. Three years passed and we still had not located him. Fifteen years later, I received a call that the authorities in California had an unidentified body and they thought it might be my brother. I provided details about him for comparison with the body. We were relieved to find out that it was not him.

Soon, twenty years had passed. Every holiday, I could see the longing in my mother's eyes for her son to be home. Then we got a call from a social worker who said my brother was in her office to get benefits. She provided an address. My brother, mother, and sister jumped in the car and drove to Los Angeles, which was eight hours away. They arrived at the address again to find it was a vacant lot. This was too much for my mother, and she began to cry uncontrollably. She was in the early stages of cancer and wondered if she would ever see her son again. She looked up and through her tears, said, "There go my baby right there." She pointed to a man in an army jacket walking briskly down the street. The man took off running, but my other brother closed in on him and called him by his nickname, "Smash, Smash, Smash." The man turned around and he was my brother. They walked back to the car where my mother and sister were.

I prayed so many prayers that my mother would be reunited with him before she went to be with the Lord. I saw my mother agonize over his leaving, blaming herself, questioning how she could have done things differently. But on that day, she held her son in her arms, screaming tears of joy. My brother was also very happy to see her. He was dressed in an army jacket, his head was partially shaved, he had dread locks, and he was clean. He took us to his home— a cardboard house that sat on the vacant lot. He explained that a man who lives near the lot let him use his bathroom to shower. He had a little grill in his home, a place to sleep, and some things he had collected. We had prepared an album with pictures of everyone, along with telephone numbers. He laughed as he looked through the pictures, seeing how everyone had changed over the years. When it was time to go, my mother began to gather his things. To her shock and amazement, he refused to leave. My mother was losing her son all over again. He was promised a ticket to come back whenever he wanted if he would just come home. He again refused to leave. My mother, powerless to force him to leave, did the only thing she could do. She bought him some food and gave him some money. She touched his face, held his hands, and hugged him ever so tightly, not knowing if this would be the last time she would have such a moment. Things did not happen as she imagined or dreamed, so she was left with the reality of the moment: he was not leaving, but they were. My mother somehow summoned the strength to get back in the car without him. Fighting to hold back her tears and feeling her heart being ripped out of her chest, she left him there to live in his cardboard house.

Several weeks later, my mother received a call. It was my brother, Matthew, and he wanted to come home. My other brother drove back to Los Angeles and brought him home. Once home, it was hard for him to live in the house, so he lived in the garage. He never closed the garage door all the way down; he always had to have it up just a little. After he had been home for a while, I asked him why he never came home. His reply was, "I thought about it a lot, but I waited so long that when I made up my mind to come home, I had forgotten where home was. I never stopped thinking about you."

Thank the Lord that my mother saw her son again before she died. He still has challenges with his mental state. He remains a gentle, loving person, and he is safe and happy now. I am glad to have my brother home. I will never give up on him.

All of my brothers graduated from high school and four of them attended college. One is deceased, one works for a city municipality, another is a nurse and another works for a granite company. We have no one to throw away. Everyone is worth saving. We do not have to go very far for ministry; we can often look within our own family and find there is kingdom work to do.

What man of you, having a hundred sheep, if he loses one of them, does not leave the ninety-nine in the wilderness, and go after the one which is lost until he finds it? And when he has found it, he lays it on his shoulders, rejoicing. And when he comes home, he calls together his friends and neighbors, saying to them, 'Rejoice with me, for I have found my sheep which was lost! [42]

My mother was a rock. She stretched every dollar she had to make sure we had something to eat and a roof over our heads. If not for her, we would have been homeless. She never drove but managed to find the least expensive places to buy food. She went to the egg farm and bought cracked eggs which were cheaper. She could take a little piece of meat and stretch it to feed eleven children. She worked hard picking figs, peaches and tomatoes. She stood for long hours at the cannery, and as she grew older, her legs caused her a lot of pain. I did everything I could to make her happy because her life had been hard. One year while working in Puerto Rico, I brought her to the island. She loved to sit and look out over the water. One day she said, "Baby, does that water go way out yonder?" I explained that we were on an island surrounded by water. She said, "Lord, have mercy, there are a lot of people with more money than I have and they have not seen this." She ate fresh pineapple and walked along the beach and had a wonderful time. I was devastated when I learned she had cancer. I cared for her down to the last day of her life.

***

My husband at the time was from a church-going family and went where a lot of his family members attended church. His Aunt Ellen was a wonderful example of a Christian woman. The church, however, practiced legalism. Women could not wear pants, go sleeveless, or wear makeup. They also could not preach, but could evangelize. They taught women to obey their husbands unconditionally. There were so many rules for women and very few for men.

---

[42] Luke 15:4-6.

I became a member of the family church and followed the rules. I taught Sunday school and helped with the children's choir. But as I studied the Word under the anointing of the Holy Spirit, I learned that I was in bondage due to the legalism practiced by the church. However, I stayed in that church until a member named Barbara went on to be with the Lord. She had breast cancer which could have been curable with surgery, but her husband told her she could not have the surgery; she should trust God instead. Barbara waited until it was too late. She died and left three beautiful children. Her husband received her retirement and other benefits, and remarried within months of her passing. How the church could encourage her to obey her husband and not seek treatment was too much for me. And for a while I was angry. Eventually, I left the family church and joined a non-denominational, spirit-filled congregation. I also began to look at my own abusive marriage. As I sat under the teaching of this new pastor, I learned that this was not God's best for me, and I made up my mind to get out of the marriage because of the abuse and adultery. After giving my husband ample time to do right, and he did not, I left. I left with very little. But when I left, I was able to walk out and not be carried out on a stretcher.

My ex-husband kept the house. I did not even have a bed to sleep on when I left him. I was terrified, but at the same time, I knew I had to trust God. I suffered a mild heart attack and while hospitalized, my ex-husband offered to let me move back into what was once our home. After I recovered, I decided to move to a nearby city. I took what I had, along with our children, thanked God I was alive and moved on. I told my ex-husband, "Keep looking up, because when you see me next, I will be on top and rising." For some reason I think he thought if he took everything, I would come back. He totally missed it. I did not care about the big house or fancy car. I left it all and started afresh. I knew that the Lord was able to do exceedingly, abundantly above all I could ask. Women, the hardest thing to do is to make the decision to leave. After that, God has your back and He will provide for you and your children.

***

For many years I worked with a government agency. During that time I travelled to the Virgin Islands, Puerto Rico, Guam, and visited Hong Kong, as well as other exotic places as part of my job. I learned to scuba dive and loved it. Everywhere I traveled I connected with a church and served as long as I was there. I taught Sunday school, as well as some adult classes. I also did community work. While on the island of Guam, I wrote and directed a play entitled, *Plenty of Time,* designed to bring the religious community together. I received a community award for my efforts.

I had a dream one night. In the dream, I was standing at a podium before a room full of women. I had no idea that God was preparing me for ministry. Life was good. I had a good government job, a beautiful home, my daughters had graduated from high school and went on to nursing school, and I was secure in my relationship with the Lord. All was well and then the bottom fell out. I was laid off; I no longer had a job. I asked myself how this could happen to me. What was I going to do? Was this a test? What had I done wrong? I decided *"though He slay me, yet will I hope in Him."*[43] I had to trust God. I had no idea what He was doing in this situation. I got up every morning with expectancy. I served even more at my church while I searched for work.

Soon it was apparent that I was running out of money and could not stay in my home. I was living off of my vacation

---

[43] Job 13:15.

pay, savings and unemployment benefits. I moved into a small apartment and rented out my house. I told the Lord, "All this stuff is yours, and just as you gave me all of these things, you can give me even more. You do what you will with your stuff." No one knew I was jobless except my pastor. My children did not know nor did my mother or brothers and sisters. I remember selling my refrigerator and buying an ice chest to keep my food cold. During that winter season of my life, I drew closer to the Lord.

I received a call to come back to work, but on a short-term assignment in Florida. I packed my bags and hit the road. Before I left, the Lord revealed to me that this would not be an ordinary assignment. We seldom know where our destiny will take us. The last thing that I expected was that I would one day be living in Georgia amongst the magnolia trees, beautiful foliage and flowers, but God had a plan and He was ordering my steps.

My assignment took me to Florida where I met Jim Manning, a federal policeman who guarded our building. He sat outside the door to my office. We talked and I attended church with him and his wife. One day he mentioned that his uncle Ron was single and he thought he and I would make a good match. I asked him to introduce us. He said his uncle lived in Atlanta. I reminded him that I lived in California and after this assignment was over, would be returning to California. He gave me a business card with Ron's name and telephone number written on the back. He said if I was ever in Atlanta I should give Ron a call. I took the business card. That night in my room, I said, "Lord, if you really want me to meet this man, you will send me to Atlanta." Two days later, my boss came to me and said, "Rebecca, they are calling you to come to Atlanta."

After being in Atlanta a couple of weeks, I decided to give my friend Jim Manning's uncle a call. The phone rang, and my heart was racing like a teenager. His son answered the telephone and took a message. Later Ron called me back. We made arrangements to meet the following night for dinner. He was a big man and quite handsome. We went to a rib shack, and then he dropped me off at my hotel. He invited me to his church and I attended with him on Sunday. Christmas was near, and his church had some activities, so I attended with him. Then one night as he dropped me off at my hotel, I stuck my head out the door and watched him as he walked to the elevator, and I heard in my spirit, "This is the man that I have set aside specifically for you." I said, "Lord, if this is the man you have set aside just for me, you must reveal it to him. If you do not reveal it to him, I will remain single." I was determined not to do what I have heard so many women have done - approach a man and tell him that the Lord said he was going to be their husband. Not me, because if the Lord revealed this to me, He would surely reveal it to Ron.

Soon my assignment was over and I headed home to California. Ron called that night to make sure I made it home safely. We talked regularly and over a period of several conversations he revealed the fact that he had feelings for me. My contract was up, and I had talked to the Atlanta office about bringing me on staff. I was told they could bring me on board in March, and it was January. So while I was in Atlanta, I secured an apartment with plans to move in March. Ron knew I had plans to relocate to Atlanta before I returned from my assignment. Our telephone calls became more intimate and we shared our feeling for each other.

One evening I received a call from Ron, and he said he needed to talk to me and was flying into Sacramento. I picked him up at the airport and we had dinner together. That night he told me, "I know you are preparing to move to Atlanta, and you are so beautiful that I want to let you know how I feel before any man in Atlanta sets eyes on you." He said, "I love you, and I want you to be my wife." I did not answer him at that time. We drove to my oldest daughter's house, and I called my youngest daughter and told her to meet me there. I introduced them to Ron and let them know he had asked me to marry him. By that time, my mother was still living and I took Ron to meet her and my brothers and sisters. My mother loved him. He is a big man and my mother at 4 feeet 11 inches had to hug him on one side and run to the other side and finish the hug. My mother had a great sense of humor. When we talked later she told me, "Baby, I would rather be an older man's sweetheart than a young man's fool." She said, "If you love that man, marry him. I hate that you will be leaving, but as long as he is good to you, I will be alright." My mother named him "Big Red" and loved him until the Lord called her home.

We spent the remainder of Ron's time in California going to some of the popular tourist areas. On his last night in the city, he asked me again to marry him and I said yes! During the next couple of days after he returned to Atlanta, I spoke with my pastor, because I had been single for quite some time, and my pastor was my covering. No matter how old you are, it is appropriate to meet with your pastor to discuss a matter as important as marriage. My pastor called and talked with Ron and said he felt that our marriage was ordained by God.

As Ron and I had only known each other for three months, our children were apprehensive. But we knew the Lord had put us together, so despite their concerns, we were married in Sacramento. It was a beautiful ceremony and we are in covenant with each other. Nothing breaks the covenant. Our children now understand that God put us together and that we are happy. They love both of us. I believe our marriage is an example of what the Lord had in mind for couples. Ron and I have been happily married for ten years. I am also thankful for the man the Lord set aside just for me. He is the love of my life. When you know you have heard from God, you must trust Him.

After marrying Ron, we attended Mount Paran Church of God where he has been a member for more than twenty years. Once a member of the church, I went right to work serving in the hospitality ministry. I then served as a part of the Women's Mentoring Ministry and assisted my Pastor's wife with teaching a women's Bible class. Later, I became the coordinator of the Christian Women in the Workplace Ministry. I knew that the call to serve women was on my life and many women have been touched and continue to be blessed through the women's ministries of the church. My husband is an Elder and I also serve as an Elder's wife.

As I served in ministry, I was led to attend Bible College. I earned an AA and BA degree in Biblical Studies and I am currently pursuing an MA degree. Being in a biblical learning environment has helped me mature in my spiritual walk.

In writing this chapter, I came to a place where I had to revisit the feelings I had for my father. I had to forgive him. Truly, genuinely forgive him. I had been walking in unforgiveness. I had this area of my heart that was scarred and I needed to mend it. It was this thing that kept me from feeling that I was worthy enough to serve, even while I was serving. It was this thing with my father that kept me from reaching the potential in ministry that God had for me. As I forgave my father, a change came over me. I had to learn to trust God and rely on Him. Do not walk around with unforgiveness in your heart. *"The Lord will accomplish what concerns you."*[44]

The love that Jesus Christ has for us is more than enough to sustain us during times of adversity. We fall in and out of love with Him and He loves us unconditionally and consistently. We cannot grow weary doing what He has called us to do because He is an endless source of strength and renewal. Stop looking at the circumstances and look at God in the circumstances. You and God, me and God, we got this, whatever it is! We trust in the name of the Lord through whatever life events come our way. The world will learn so much more from us when they see how we act when things are not perfect. Even when things are at the darkest, remember God can see perfectly for He is the Light. We must be obedient to do what God has called us to do in the

---

[44] Psalm 138:8.

Reclaiming Who We Are
(One Woman's Reflections on a Womanist Theology)

By T. G. Monroy

My formation as a theologian came at the cost of suicide. The untimely death of my ex-husband forced me to take responsibility for my past, present, and future. Because of Rodney's death, I immediately understood life can be a friend or a foe. Gratefully, my relationship with God taught me the gift of life. The ability to interpret the lessons learned through the use of an academic paradigm added to my value of understanding life experiences. Adopting a womanist approach to theology gave me a method to construct my interpretation of spirituality, embodiment, community, and mental health as it pertains to moving forward with my theological development.

The continuum that the field of womanist theology fortifies becomes a magnifying mechanism that enhances and gives validity to the African American woman's experience. God's existence in and through her becomes evident. This qualifies her to know that she is a unique creation and a part of a totality that belongs to God. In that vein, my road to becoming a formidably informed theologian requires a workable understanding of existence which becomes a byproduct of life occurrence/experience with attention paid to "sexism, classism, and racism."[45] Formidably is used with the

---

[45] Jacquelyn Grant, *White Women's Christ and Black Women's Jesus: Feminist Christology and Womanist Response* (Atlanta: Scholars Press, 1989), 209.

intent to understand the abusive, discounted, malicious, terror-filled road known to the African American race in America.

Despite the torrid history that looms over the African American woman in particular, there is a desire and need to live with self understanding and validation of her story. That understanding surpasses her being; the entire African American community relies upon her. The reliance upon her readily meets the response of acceptance and encompasses every thing she finds dear as she is responsible for those she loves. African American women are known for "...taking care of and covering for everybody with very little thanks."[46]

Through her struggles the African American woman has surmised an existence of God beyond the four walls of the church. "Church and God are two different things...God is not just in churches; God's everywhere and in everything. Sometimes churches are the hardest place to find Him."[47] For all intent and purposes, much of the spiritual awareness and/or God consciousness known to African Americans have transpired long before we were introduced to the Bible.[48] It is no secret that since we knew ourselves, we knew God.

The many names of God have by no means confused African Americans nor deterred a people away from seeking comfort at the hands of the Almighty. The songs, practices, and

---

[46] Anthony Watson, "Mary Don't You Weep: Becoming My Mother's Son," in *My Soul is a Witness: African American Women's Spirituality*, ed. Gloria Wade-Gayles (Boston: Beacon Press 2002), 57.

[47] Paul Woods, "Spirit Never Fails," in *My Soul is a Witness: African American Women's Spirituality*, ed. Gloria Wade-Gayles (Boston: Beacon Press 2002), 112.

[48] Jacquelyn Grant, *White Women's Christ and Black Women's Jesus: Feminist Christology and Womanist Response"*(Atlanta: Scholars Press, 1989), 211.

prayers from my youth are testament to God's existence. I can remember a time when my momma would be hanging out clothes while talking with God. She would have a stern look on her face. Throughout the years, I have come to know that my momma was full of purpose as she hung out the clothes and toiled in her yard spending quality time with the Lord.

Momma was always "planting and burying" something in the yard from the time I was a child.[49] I can't remember anything she enjoyed more. Her work in the yard was nothing short of a labor of love. There was a noticeable difference in her demeanor entering the yard to work and her demeanor after the work was finished; the yard was spiritually therapeutic. When Momma was in the yard toiling, we all knew not to disturb her for any reason. On those rare occasions that someone dared call on her while she was in the yard, her shortness of voice indicated agitation. It was evident that beckoning her took time away from her joy. Whatever she planted grew and was to be admired. I often wondered why she spent so much time in the dirt. I now know that was her altar. I never knew the magnitude of peace she found in communion with God as she dug in the dirt.

The "...relationship between oppression and theological symbolism" of African American spirituality is encapsulated by faith.[50] The old Negro spiritual *Nobody Knows the Trouble I've Seen* is a true testament of the plight of African American women. Any anthology of African American existence proves

---

[49] Fleda Mask Jackson, "In the Morning, When I Rise: My Hands in Spiritual Soil," in *My Soul is a Witness: African American Women's Spirituality*, ed. Gloria Wade-Gayles (Boston: Beacon Press 2002), 54.
[50] Stephanie Mitchem, *Introducing Womanist Theology* (New York: Orbis Books, 2002), 71.

the un-measurable challenges and hardships known to a people which could only be overcome by divine intervention.

It is impossible to acknowledge African American women theologically or otherwise and not take note of their spirituality and faith. Walking the road towards theological scholasticism is a mandate to give voice to the African American experience from the perspective of women as it relates to being created in the image of God.

In her lecture on *Womanist Spirituality*, Dr. Maisha Handy stated, "Theology perpetuates a lot of oppression."[51] I find this assertion to be accurate. It is troubling to consider that human beings would use God to perpetuate their personal agendas that yield the end result of oppression. If we are all made in the image of God, then it stands to reason we are all created equal. The only way to combat spiritual impropriety as it relates to the African American woman is through the proliferation of truth by giving voice to our story uplifted as theological symbolism. Symbolism means significance. The idea of the African American's voice as insignificant in arenas outside the Black community needs to change, extracting the value of our experience to benefit humanity. We have something to contribute!

Without a shadow of a doubt, had my ex-husband remained alive, I would not have answered my call to ministry or embraced my "picky" hair and size. God affirmed the beauty within me, existentially, and extended my life to serve God's people holistically with unconditional love. Beyond the incident of loss that made me answer my call to be a minister some years ago, I was on a quest to know myself. I questioned how my ex-husband could check into a hotel room and kill

---

[51] Maisha Handy, *Womanist Spirituality,* (class lecture, ITC, February 4, 2010).

himself. He separated himself and died alone. I did not realize his degree of despair. Were the mean comments he made toward me a sign of his self hatred? I went to the funeral for the sole purpose of making sure it was him. Years of fear, the burning down of my car, tampering with my credit, strange men peeping in my window as a scare tactic, and the feeling of anxiety were all reasons enough for me to make sure it was him in the casket.

Rodney was a terror in his last days. I was forced to look at myself, investigate my life. Who am I? Where did all of this trouble come from? What part did I play? How did I make such bad choices? Would I have been better off had I not left the relationship and lived a lie? Would he have still been alive had I stayed? Was his suicide indicative of a potential homicide? Over the years, I have asked these questions of myself. I have not answered all of them, however, enough of them have been answered that I have since moved forward. I am now blessed with a supportive second husband and a ten year old son. God gave me a new lease on life that took the negative experience of a premature marriage and used it as a frame of reference to be present with others in hardships.

The resilience that I portrayed in my life is more common than uncommon amongst African American women. The first thing I did when I got free was cut my hair and go natural. So I could certainly relate to the stories in *Naked: Black Women Bare All About Their Skin, Hair, Hips, Lips, and Other Parts*. There was a time when I did not "feel completely at home in my own skin."[52] I hated when men would stand on the side of the street and make lewd comments as I passed by. I had

---

[52] Ayana Byrd, "Piropos," in *Naked: Black Women Bare All About Their Skin, Hair, Hips, Lips, and Other Parts*, Ayana Byrd and Akiba Solomon, eds. (New York: Perigee Trade, 2005), 17.

witnessed so many of them behave insensitively that I was not interested in their company. One of the reasons I married young was for protection from the world. Wearing a wedding ring gave me a reason to be nonresponsive without receiving as much verbal abuse from men.

My mom never talked about sexuality. She was not the kind of woman that I could approach about boys. I never had a boyfriend in high-school. In fact, Rodney was the only guy I took home and introduced as my boyfriend. We met in college. My dad told me explicitly, "don't bring no white boy to my house." He must have known my taste early on; I married the first time to please my parents. The second marriage was to please me.

I was bigger and taller than most of the girls I grew up with. Height was a curse in those days. Thus books became my friends because they spoke a different language. They did not focus on my flaws. I spent hours reading. The time spent reading gave me an excuse to be reclusive.

African American girls never saw me as a contender when it came to the boys; they automatically counted me out. I was about seventeen years old when a white man said to me, "your body is a piece of artwork." It blew my mind. All I had ever heard before then was comments like "fat girl", "big girl", and "big momma". Interestingly enough, I did not begin to appreciate my beauty until I was about twenty-five years old. The woman I have become has found appreciation in my outer and inner beauty. The other day I was in the grocery store and a *sistah* was staring at me. She said, "I love the color of your hair." I was perplexed having forgotten that my hair was fire red; I wondered why she was staring at me. She expressed interest in having my color hair and admitted that she wanted to free herself and go natural also. I walked her to find the hair care products. I was glad to share sisterly love and the box of hair dye with her.

The collective healing that bell hooks speaks about was actualized by sharing the box of hair dye. The dye was representative of the notion that "we have to be about the business of inventing all manner of images and representations that show us the way we want to be and are" with the freedom to share with each other.[53] Agreeably, "it is difficult to find affirming images of black femaleness within white-supremacist patriarchal society."[54] Today, I am aware of the obligation to embrace, encourage, and love my sisters and self. It is a mandate. There is no insignificant occasion. Every opportunity should be seized to affirm beauty inwardly and outwardly.

Beauty is not determined by sexuality; all of God's creation is beautiful. I am especially sensitive to the oppression faced by homosexuals. That was partially why I went to Bible College and seminary to study further God's Word on sexuality. The assertion made in *Daring to Speak* that "the oppression that affects Black gay people, female and male, is pervasive, constant, and not abstract."[55] Some of us die because of it; it is alarming! My ex-husband was one of those people that died because of it. He experimented with homosexuality after our separation and ultimately could not live with himself and committed suicide.

---

[53] bell hooks, *Sisters of the Yam: Black Women and Self-Recovery* (Boston: Southend Press, 1993), 83.
[54] Ibid, 83.
[55] Kelly Brown Douglas, "Daring to Speak: Womanist Theology and Black Sexuality," in *Embracing the Spirit: Womanist Perspective on Hop, Salvation and Transformation*, Emilie M. Townes, ed. (Maryknoll, NY: Orbis Books, 2001), 243.

One of my professors, Dr. Margaret Aymer changed my perspective on theology and made me feel a sense of security and familiarity I had not experienced before. I have viewed theology from a "hands off approach" in the past. There was always admiration for the fight African American women won to have a theological voice but I misunderstood the true nature of sisterhood. Aymer's explanation of theology starting from an epistemological rather than an ontological basis, in her experience, helped me to better understand my own formation as a person and scholar. I quickly realized that "womanism" was more inclusive than exclusive, and woman of color have undeniable similarities despite our countries of origin. I have come to know that regardless of a Black woman's place of origin, we share the experience of un-acceptance in various ways.

Being perceived by others as a "woman out of order" often times left me with feelings of desertion and abandonment until recently. But my feelings of sadness, resentment, dismay, and anger towards the actions done in and by people in my community has been changed through my seminary education. Community is defined as all of God's creation. Often times we think of ourselves as just individuals, separated from one another, whereas we are connected to the whole of humanity. It was not until I began to embrace my life story in totality that I realized *Ubuntu* exists. Archbishop Desmond Tutu offered the following description of *Ubuntu*:

> A person with *Ubuntu* is open and available to others, affirming of others, does not feel threatened that others are able and good, for he or she has a proper self-assurance that comes from knowing that he or she belongs in a greater whole and is diminished when

others are humiliated or diminished, when others are tortured or oppressed.[56]

As a child, I had no idea that my community was looking out for me the best they could. I just thought they were a bunch of mean miserable people. I now know they had my best interest at heart. It pained my mom and big sister to consider the difficulty I would face throughout life if my response to adversity remained that of tears; their only thought was people would take advantage of my weakness. They did their best at "armoring" me so I could withstand the challenges of being an African American female in a prejudiced, sexist society.[57]

My mom was the first person that came to my mind as I read *Women Out of Order: Risking Change and Creating Care in a Multicultural World*. She is a Geechee woman who has been known to stand her ground despite opposition. Her personhood embodies strength. Despite the numerous physical altercations witnessed between her and dad, the first time I can remember seeing my mom cry was a while after my brother Lil Harold was murdered. My mom and dad fought like soldiers, but they were not physically abusive to their children. The image of "Strong Black Woman" depicts to a tee my mom's actions at the loss of her son; she did not breakdown until weeks after my brother's burial. When she did breakdown, it was in the kitchen, with only immediate family in the house.[58]

---

[56] Tutu, Desmond, *No Future without Forgiveness* (New York: Doubleday, 1999).

[57] Ibid, 49.

[58] Beverly Wallace, "A Womanist Legacy of Trauma, Grief, and Loss: Reframing the Notion of the Strong Black Woman," in *Women Out of Order: Risking Change and Creating Care in a Multicultural World*, Jeanne Stevenson-Moessner and Teresa Snorton, eds.(Minneapolis: Fortress Press, 2009), 48.

She thought it weakness to show raw emotions that deemed her vulnerable. I did not find her actions odd until now because she was normal according to the Black women I was familiar with.

My mom and sister's interpretation of strength in womanhood demanded I walk in that same strength they exemplified; a show of tears was an automatic indication that I was not handling the situation at hand but rather the situation had gotten the best of me. In my mom's mind, without masking my true feelings, life would have its dismal way with me. I have come to realize my sadness, anger, and contempt for the Black community was largely due to my mom's strong Black persona. Her avoidance of sensitivity and vulnerability became my frame of reference, which I often times interpreted as unfeeling and uncaring.

As soon as possible, I left my parents house for college to escape the environment. I did not want to be considered a hard, stern-faced woman. I devalued the sense of who my community was because of a misinterpretation of what I thought it was. I had been exposed to various environments and began to make comparisons. Unfortunately, the non-Black communities I compared the Black community to were not equal; they did not have to navigate their way through the bottom rung of self degradation and slavery induced self hatred.

In her lecture on *Womanist Community*, Dr. Itihari Toure taught that interconnectedness and interdependence are natural states of community as illustrated in the *Ubuntu* philosophy.[59] Her interpretation of community gave me a frame of reference that explains a lot about who I am in response to the disconnect I have struggled with for many years.

---

[59] Itihari Toure, *Womanist Community*, (class lecture, ITC, March 25, 2010).

I had felt betrayed by the Black community. I felt when it was time to stand up for what was right, my people abandoned me. I began to see members of my community as opportunists that refused to fight the good fight but were open to reap the rewards of another's fight. Due to the disappointments I had endured, I viewed community as a function that I could participate in at will and not as an essential part of my being. I became frustrated by the obvious masking within the African American community. Dr. Toure helped me to understand that my issue with the Black community was a reality not to be overlooked. She introduced a new idea called the "mis-function" of community,[60] which is when community does not function the way it is designed to function according to *Ubuntu*. She also helped me to discover my value within the community in a way that I had not realized before. Dr. Toure helped me to understand that my existence really is attributed to all that exists about me. If I continue to view community as a function and not as an integral part of my being, I hinder my give/take role within the community. As the African proverb states: "*I truly am because we are.*" Despite the challenges I have faced, I am better equipped to own my place in community at forty than when I was in my twenties.

My twenties were the most challenging years of my life. I was faced with situations that could have easily caused mental illness. On one hand, I wanted to please my mother and sister. On the other hand, there was something inside of me that demanded I please self. Needless to say, I was true to myself. The plans my ex-husband and family held for my life were unimportant. In hindsight, I have the assurance that the Holy Spirit was making intervention for me and keeping me out of harm's way. Life was happening and I did not have many

---

[60] Ibid.

experiences to extrapolate solutions from. Looking back, the frustration I felt had more to do with fears from inexperience.

I was in a situation of suffering. I reluctantly married my college sweetheart. Rodney showed signs of mental illness early in our relationship. Rodney's public image and home life were opposite. His public image was professional and family-oriented. At home, Rodney was physically and verbally abusive; he was an alcoholic and a marijuana drug dealer. My family regarded him as the perfect husband; I was the spoiled, complaining, unappreciative wife. My sister thought Rodney was God's gift. Part of the problem was that Rodney was the embodiment of a slot machine that "kicked" out money to family and friends. His ability to give money was more beneficial to them than my seemingly unwarranted complaining.

Although my ex-husband was an actor of sorts, I knew him like the back of my hand. I now know my ability to "know" is relative to the gift of discernment. I regularly approached him with questions and assertions. It was not until five years after our separation and three days before he committed suicide, Rodney called me and confirmed that my suspicions were true. I will never forget the conversation we had on that day.

Before realization of my gifts, there were times I almost bought into the comments that suggested that I was mentally ill. My actions were counter-cultural. What I mean by counter-cultural is this: I did not buy into the "Mammy" stereotype; not for a moment. This ideology depicts an African American woman in a paradoxical role as good-natured, unselfishly nurturing and caring for others while at the same time unfeminine, strong willed, domineering and neglectful of her own personhood. My sister's purpose for calling me "spoiled" and "selfish" heavily rested on the notion of my unwillingness to be "...infinite resources for others, always strong in the face of adversity and having no need to care for myself."[61]

My heart goes out to women that buy into the "Mammy" stereotype. Perhaps this was the cause of many disagreements between me and my strong mother and sister. I resented the arrogance of the idea "...that something in African-American women's experience predisposes them to this form of symptom expression."[62]

Who asked to be viewed as "Mammy"? I sure didn't. The experience of African American women is not something we created for ourselves. Like many other things, the construct was created by society and assigned to us. I prefer the construct God created for me. God has created me with a sense of freedom and liberty. I don't believe God created us to live in bondage. I believe God's act of creation was an act of liberation. God didn't create one type of individual. God took the time to create different ethnicities, skin colors, and cultures with various traditions. I view God's creation as a celebratory act. Therefore, there is no need to sacrifice the very essence of who God created us to be to please others.

***

In her lecture *Womanist Mental Health and Wellness,* Dr. Marjorie Lewis affirmed my objections to being called selfish. She made the assertion, "...be a separatist for health."[63] She was preaching to the choir. My ex-husband did not end

---

[61] Ibid, 239.

[62] Ibid, 240.

[63] Marjorie Lewis, *Womanist Mental Health and Wellness* (class lecture, ITC, April 15, 2010).

our tumultuous marriage, I did. Rodney went to work on Halloween, 2006, and I left without telling him. I made one of the best decisions ever! I refused to throw away my personhood to be in relationship with him.

Dr. Lewis also raised the issue of mental health versus mental illness. In the Black community, we tend to "focus more on mental illness than mental health."[64] Could it be we dismiss the importance of mental health due to the traumatic experiences endured communally as a way to forget? Sacrifice and suffering are common place among African Americans. "African-American women have a tradition of bearing their suffering as if it is inevitable and sometimes as if it is a manifestation of their ethnic identity."[65]

I wrestle with the injustice African American women suffer. We have been subjected to oppression and mistreatment, many times, because we are Black. It is only a blessing from God that we possess resilience that defies all odds. Beyond the stigmas placed upon us by society at large, we often times suffer at the hands of our own community. I am disturbed by the perpetuation of bondage Black women face on a daily basis. The most disturbing notion for me is many women are not in a position to voice their suffering and many receive inadequate support. When I became vocal about my ex-husband's abuse and suggested he get mental help, I was regarded as the villain. Immediately, I was told, "You find problems with everybody." I was attacked for making "unrealistic" demands on Rodney's personhood. I ignored the

---

[64] Ibid.

[65] Cheryl Thompson, "African American Women and Moral Masochism," in *Psychotherapy with African American Women: Innovations in Psychodynamic Perspectives and Practice*, Leslie Jackson and Beverly Greene, eds. (New York: The Guilford Press, 2000), 240.

attacks and got the help I needed to break free. Granted, it was difficult to overcome the challenges that came with ending the relationship. The greatest outcome has been the protection of my mental health.

I yet struggle with a number of questions. Is the stigma of mental illness in the African American community an indication of communal denial? The trauma suffered by African Americans suggests there is a great need for mental health awareness. Until women recognize the importance of mental health, they will continue to fall prey to self sacrifice as the norm. Through awareness, we become empowered to break free from the bondage of public opinion.

Mental health and wellness are important to live a fulfilled life.

***

Spirituality, embodiment, community, and mental health are all paths to a fulfilled life. God is the author of life. There is no need to act the script; live the script. Life experiences do not outweigh God's power. Whatever it is, it has the potential to become better. It is not uncommon for negative situations to serve as a springboard to the delicacies of life that only few get to behold. Be one of the few that have learned how to become intoxicated by the gift of life.

Two suggestions for praxis:

1. <u>Keep living; don't concede to the circumstances of life</u>. Create new circumstances with God's help. My past has made room for the present and future. I am better

equipped to successfully manage life situations through the experiences gained along the way. I now know that challenges have the potential to make me wiser.

2. <u>Embrace life as a friend rather than a foe</u>. To embrace life as a friend opens the door to embrace God's creation as "friend" and not "enemy". Embrace others knowing they too have lived through uneventful situations. Kindness is a gift people will happily receive unwrapped. They will place the gift of kindness on the mantle of their hearts.

PART 3

Called to Lead

"What is so special about you that God moves heaven and earth to see about you? Why does the Spirit work so hard to get and keep your attention focused on God? It's because God loves and has great things in store for you. It is because God has great plans for you. Already the Lord has a vested interest in you. You can't keep dodging the Holy Spirit, pretending not to hear or understand what God wants with you. You have an assignment!"

Dr. Cynthia L. Hale
I'm a Piece of Work

Forgetting the Past
By Natalie Brannon-Lipede

"Brethren, I count not myself to have apprehended: but this one thing I do; forgetting those things which are behind, and reaching forth unto those things which are before, I press toward the mark for the prize of the high calling of God in Christ Jesus."[66]

To all of the young girls who are growing-up without fathers and positive male role models, I dedicate this article to you and to the many young women in ministry who struggle with not being affirmed by others in leadership within the church. My desire is that as you come to know God in a deeper and more personal relationship, your sense of self -worth will increase as He reveals who He created you to be. I pray that you will let go of all the negative thoughts and words that have come from others or even yourself—that they will leave and never return. I pray that you live in wholeness knowing that you have a heavenly Father who loves you in ways that you never dreamed possible and that through reading my story you to will realize that you have a voice and you will be silent no more.

***

Both my parents were really young when I was born. Shortly after the birth of my younger brother their relationship was severed. My father sang in a popular group at that time and the group was invited to perform on the Ed Sullivan Show. As a result, my father was offered a contract from Motown, but

---

[66] Philippians 13:13-14.

not the other members of the group. For him, this was the chance of a lifetime. Sadly, my father did not accept the contractual offer and continued to do small music gigs. With two young children at home and no means of supporting them except by doing small gigs every now and then, my mother was devastated. This is the main reason why my parent's relationship did not last. But my father was also mentally abusive. Neither of them remarried.

For years I remember imagining and hoping that the two would reunite and we would be a family again. My mother never spoke negatively about my father and neither did she prevent us from seeing him. We usually spent two weekends each month with our father's parents. Occasionally he would stop by to see us, but he never had much to say and that did not matter much—I just wanted to see my daddy. Over time, his visits were less frequent and eventually he only visited us every three, four or five years. During the early eighties when Atlanta child murders were going on my father came to visit us and he was seen talking to my brother. The Neighborhood Watch person did not recognize him and called the police. When the police asked my brother who he was, my brother did not know him. When I came home from school the policeman questioned me: "Is that your father? How long has it been since you have seen him? Can you recognize him if you see him again?" I answered the questions. Then I followed the policeman to the car and peered through his car window. "Yes, that is my daddy," I said.

By the age of ten I knew my parents were not going to reunite and I was angry with my father for leaving us. I was lonely and afraid. Where was he when I needed him? I needed him to help me, to hold me, to protect me, and to save me. By that time, my mother had divorced my father. One day my class visited the school's library and I came across a book by Judy Blume, "*Are You There God? It's Me Margaret.*" In this book, a girl needed answers and she turned to God for help. I identified with this girl; I too could find help from God if I talked to him and that is what I did. Near the apartment that we lived was a small brick church, Mt. Sinai Baptist Church. It was so close to our apartment that we could almost see what was going on inside. Every Sunday morning my mother would get me up and make sure that I was dressed. Then she would give me an offering for Sunday school and one for the main service then watch me from our dining room window as I walked inside the church with my Bible in my hand. After service I would see her sitting near the window as I walked back home. She anxiously waited for me to tell her what the preacher talked about as if I was a messenger or something. Of the four people who lived in our house, I was the only one that went to church. So one day I got up the nerve to ask, "Why don't Roe (my brother) go to church?" she replied, "Because he is a boy." I did not quite understand her answer, but I knew not to ask anything else and that was the end of the discussion.

Being the youngest of three girls in my family was also difficult at times. I was never included in girl talk or secrets among the other two girls and spent most of my time playing with my brother and male cousins. My mother was what people referred to as strict back then. My boundary for play was no further than the front porch. As I grew older, like many kids, I tested those boundaries and would leave the porch and return before her bus pulled up to the corner. I was quite fond of one girl in the neighborhood and would go to her house and talk with her. She was a little older but she did not mind allowing me to tag along with her. One day we walked to the gas station/convenience store and there she met her friend. He was sitting in a canary yellow Cadillac. He was beautiful with thick black hair, pearly white teeth, and deep dimples on each side. We stood and talked for a few minutes and then walked back to her house. We did that on several occasions, but she never talked about her relationship with him and he never said anything to me except "hello". He always seemed kind and spoke in soft tones. I remember thinking, "I wish he was my daddy." After a few months my friend was expecting a child and our walks ended that summer. Rumor had it that he was a pimp. I recently shared that story with my mother and we both laughed. I now understand why she was so protective but, even when she was nowhere around God the Father was protecting me all the time.

During my adolescent years, around age twelve, me, my brother, and my mother were invited to a camp meeting service and when the alter call was given I immediately left my seat and stood with others who also wanted salvation. Moments later I was joined by my mother who re-dedicated her life to Christ that very night. I was very zealous and desired to be in church whenever service was held. I knew my mother was tired from working so I would make sure that my brother and I did our chores, ate dinner, completed homework, and were dressed and ready to go to church—even when she did not want to. I even prepared her clothes. Going to church and reading the Bible helped me to grow strong in most areas, but I struggled with unforgiveness. One day the pastor preached on forgiveness. I tried hard to think of people that I needed to forgive and all I could see was the face of my father. After some time I had forgotten about him because I was engrossed in church and my own life. But as I began to grow strong in God, I was reminded of the unforgiveness I had towards him. The more I prayed and asked God to help me forgive him the angrier I became. This period lasted for years. I hated Father's Day and any mention of him or anything related to fathers. I prayed for God to take the unforgiveness away but it stayed there and I could not get rid of it. I would get over it but as soon as something reminded me of him, I regressed.

I dealt with this anger alone—no one knew but my mother and she helped as best as she could. I would seclude myself away from people until those feelings of depression subsided. In 1986, I graduated from high school and when invitations were mailed out one was sent to my father; again he was not present as he had not been in the years past.

During my college years I continued to struggle with depression but not as much I did when I was younger. As I got older the bouts of depression did not last as long. I tried hard not to even think about my experiences. Eventually, I grew numb to it. One day browsing in the bookstore I came across a book titled *Succeeding Against All Odds* by the late founder and editor of Ebony magazine. I bought the book and it inspired me because I felt as if all odds were against me. I was able to connect with the man in the book as he shared his life's struggles and successes. After reading that book I came across other books that helped me with my own challenges.

At the age of twenty-two, I found myself in a dilemma—I was dating a young man named Charles Lipede, from Nigeria. Things were getting serious. I knew I had issues and did not want to bring another person into my situation making his life miserable. I explained my situation and told him that I understood if he did not want to pursue the relationship any further. I did not know what I wanted in a man or what to expect from one. But God had chosen and predestined this man for me. For he was everything I needed and everything God wanted for me. One day we visited the Auburn Festival in Atlanta where my father was scheduled to perform. When we saw each other, we embraced and I introduced Charles to him. Then we walked and talked and I knew in my heart that I had forgiven this man that had once caused me so much pain. Charles and I married December 5, 1992.

Moving from the pains of neglect from my father has helped me in ministry. In essence the Holy Spirit had spoken to me ever since I was a little girl. *"Before I formed thee in the belly I knew thee; and before thou comest forth out of the womb I sanctified thee, and I ordained thee a prophet unto the nations."*[67] But the need to be affirmed by others played a major role in my failure to acknowledge the call of God upon my life. For years I waited for a preacher or some person in leadership to place a stamp of approval on me.

Fear of being rejected also affected my position as a woman in ministry. I knew that I was called to preach the Word of God even before becoming a member of a church. My upbringing had taught me a lot about prayer and faith, which helped me to build a relationship with God. I was always willing to do the work of the Lord, but I will admit I had doubts about how He was going to make it happen. I experienced rejection, sadly, in the church. To begin with, my family background did not fit the packaging of an evangelist or preacher. My mother was single and raised two children; she worked in a hair salon and catered small functions on the side. She was a lay person and faithful choir member, but she was never called to lead in worship or anything like that. So to even speculate that God would choose me was not thought of. But I was fortunate to be in a church where women evangelists visited regularly and conducted revivals. I would sit on the front row of the church and hold onto every word that was spoken.

---

[67] Jeremiah 1:5.

These women brought encouragement and hope to the young and old alike. I was among those who wished that one day I could do what they were doing. I recall Evangelist Maria Gardner's story of neglect and being a single mom. What inspired me the most was her sincerity both in and out of the pulpit. There was also Pastor Ernestine Reems from Los Angeles, California. What I remember most about her was her boldness in the pulpit. The youngest among the women was Evangelist Sandra Riley who has been instrumental in the strengthening of our generation. I have been blessed by the presence of so many wonderful women in ministry who has dared to "lift their voice" and I am eternally grateful to them.

***

Just before completing high school I had decided to attend Oral Roberts University (ORU), but things happened with my paper work and instead I attended one of the local colleges and earned a degree in education. I was ordained into the ministry later, but did not pursue the call to ministry and was content and comfortable singing in the music ministry. My desire to serve Him intensified as I served in the music ministry and in Sunday school and Vacation Bible School. I was very supportive of the ministries that I served, but I needed more and I began to seek God. As I lead the praise and worship services, unusual things began to happen. The Spirit of God would overtake me and along with the praise team I would find myself kneeling worshipping God. These events began to take place more frequently than not and I was feeling uncomfortable as if I was causing a disturbance—but knowing that it was not me but the Holy Spirit that was upon me.

One Sunday after the morning worship service I sent the children home with my husband and I drove alone. As I drove, with no particular destination in mind, a deep sense of conviction came over me and my eyes filled with tears. First, I repented to God for the way that I had served Him. I heard myself holler out, "I'm sorry Lord!" I began to loose control and frantically turned into a parking lot. I did not know where I was and it did not matter. I realized that I had pleased everybody and did everything others wanted except God. I calmed down finally and I looked up at the building where I had parked. When I looked up, I saw that it was one of the local seminaries. I began to weep again and say, "Yes Lord I will go." I knew that the Holy Spirit had directed me to this place as a sign that the Lord wanted me to go back to school, and to a place where I would learn of Him. Miraculously, God had brought me back to what His desires were for me years ago when I first applied to a seminary. I had forsaken God's will for my own and now it was time to do His will. The very next day I called Beulah Heights University and within a few days I received admission information in the mail. I mailed the application; it was already too late to apply for financial aid, but I was determined to register even if I had to pay my tuition out of pocket.

While going through all the processes of admissions and registration we had several visitors to speak at the church and the Lord, through the Holy Spirit, spoke words of prophecy through each one to me all pertaining to what God was getting ready to do concerning me. I knew that these words could only come from God because absolutely nobody knew about what I had experienced but God. A short while after those messages, I was licensed as an evangelist. One of the prophetic words was to embrace my pastor because that would become my destiny. In January 2010, I became the executive pastor of The Rock Christian Center in Lithonia, Georgia. Praise God!

Although my life has taken this journey of neglect and rejection I realize that I am not alone. I was raised by a single mother and do not know the joys of having an earthly father, but God has continued to prove his love for me every day. I speak passionately to those who share similar experiences and find it difficult to live past the hurt. I say to you, I understand. Like many other women, I was hopeless, helpless, and depressed. But I found help and hope in Christ Jesus.

As a little girl I came to know God and my faith grew through prayer and reading the Bible. I came to realize that all of those times when I walked to church alone—I was not alone. Through role models—that I watched from a distance—God taught me about being in relationship with Him. Through reading books about people who overcame obstacles—God taught me about being all He intended me to be. But He also gave me the patience to wait and allow Him to establish me. Now that I am mature it gives me no greater pleasure than to encourage the next generation to do the same. The most important lesson that I had to learn was forgiveness. Once I genuinely forgave my earthly father, my heavenly Father accepted me and adopted me into His family. My father and I do not have the kind of relationship I desired as a child and probably never will, but I do love and pray for him. Forgiveness feels good like a breath of fresh air. I rarely have thoughts of those childhood experiences and they only come to surface when it is necessary to minister to someone. I often share some of these experiences in the pulpit and it never amazes me at the number of young women who greet me at the end of the service or some other place and share similar stories or are seeking advice on how to deal with their relationship with their fathers.

In the future I would like to have a youth empowerment program for girls ranging in ages between ten through eighteen years old. I would especially like the program to target those girls whose fathers are absent in the home. My ministry is inclusive of all family types but God has gifted me with a special anointing to young women who are intelligent, beautiful, talented and special, but do not understand who God has created them to become. Through life's circumstances I now have the self-esteem and identity of who I am in Christ Jesus and I wake up each day knowing and looking for the young woman God will put in my path to assist as she strives towards her destiny. I am privileged to do for others what many women have done for me. Sometimes it is not what I say that determines my influence, but more often what I do. More than anything I want to be an example for my two daughters, Patience and Destiny, and show them what it means to be a Christian. I want to exemplify how Christ uses women and men in ministry regardless of gender. As I share the gospel with others I pray that my children will also adhere to the message that Christ commands and that some day as they are lead by the Spirit of God they (along with our son) will answer the call and lift their voices to share the message of Christ to their generation.

Answering the Call
By Wanda Crowder

"Wanda, Wanda," a voice called to me one night as I was sleeping. When I heard the voice; it sounded audible, and it woke me up.

"Feed my sheep," the voice said. It was strong, very stern, commanding and powerful.

"Who are you?" I asked,

"I am the Lord your God." At first I was frightened. I did not know what to think.

"Feed my sheep," the voice said again. I trembled, my body stiffened as I gradually accepted who was actually summoning me.

The next morning I asked my husband if he had heard anything the night before, he said he had not. When I explained what had happened he said, "I think you need to wait on that."

That morning I was anxious to get to work to talk with my prayer partner. When I shared it with her she said, "Praise the Lord, that's wonderful!" But when I asked her what it meant she said, "Go back and pray. The Lord will reveal it to you." I did not know if I should be excited or frightened, I believe I was both.

I did not speak to my pastor about it right away because I was seeking clarity on what it meant. But the voice of God kept after me "feed my sheep," I could not get away from it, but I did not understand exactly what He meant. So I prayed and studied Scripture in John 21:15-17:

So when they had eaten breakfast, Jesus said to Simon Peter, "Simon, son of Jonah, do you love Me more than these?" He said to Him, "Yes, Lord; You know that I love You." He said to him, "Feed My lambs." He said to him again a second time, "Simon, son of Jonah, do you love Me?" He said to Him, "Yes, Lord; You know that I love You." He said to him, "Tend My sheep." He said to him the third time, "Simon, son of Jonah, do you love Me?" Peter was grieved because He said to him the third time, "Do you love Me?" And he said to Him, "Lord, You know all things; You know that I love You." Jesus said to him, "Feed My sheep."

A few days later we went with the pastor to a church in Fort Valley Georgia, I sat there and as he was preaching I heard this whisper of a voice saying again and again, "Feed my sheep. Feed my sheep. Feed my sheep." It was so haunting that I got up and walked out of the church. At this point I was still unsure that this was a divine summons to preach. Again on Easter Sunday, as my pastor was preaching, he left his original text and started talking about Peter's conversation with Jesus after his resurrection. As he spoke the words, "Peter, do you love me?" I became very uneasy. When the words rolled off of his tongue, "Feed my sheep," a rush came over me and I was again shaken and began to cry. I took it that this was my nudge from God to speak with my pastor. So I made an appointment with him. As I arrived at this office, I saw another minister there who had always given me a rough time. She waited outside while I talked with him. I felt intimidated.

As I began to open up and share what had happened I broke into tears, my pastor looked at me emotionless. He told me that I needed to prepare a statement for the church announcing my call into the ministry. When the time came, I stood before the church and announced that I was just another "voice crying in the wilderness prepare ye the way of the Lord." The next step in this process was to prepare a sermon to preach before the congregation.

I was excited but at the same time afraid as I began to wait before the Lord seeking the Scripture that I should preach. Eventually there were two Scriptures: John 1:1: *"In the beginning was the word and the Word was with God and the Word was God."* This text is speaking about how Jesus came to earth being the incarnate Word—the Word made flesh.[68] The second text was Luke 4:18-19:

> *The Spirit of the Lord is upon me because he anointed me to preach the gospel to the poor. He has sent me to proclaim release to the captives and recovery of sight to the blind. To set free those who are down trodden, to proclaim the favorable year of the Lord.* [69]

This was Jesus' mission statement as he set about to bring about healing, restoration, and provision, and win people back to His Father. He is summoning both men and women to do the same.

Answering the call is not easy but it is definitely fulfilling. On the road to ministry I have faced many obstacles. Truthfully I did not expect such difficulties to come. I always thought that surrendering my life to Christ would mean smooth sailing—no obstacles, no crises, no storms. But I am thankful for every difficulty I have endured because without

---

[68] John 1:14.
[69] Luke 4:18-19.

them there would be no spiritual growth. I desire to continue growing—never quitting.

As I write this article, I can think of several obstacles that I dealt with:

1. Fear of failure. When I first realized God was indeed calling me, I felt like Isaiah when he said, "*Woe is me for I am undone.*"[70] I immediately started to focus on my inadequacies, and wrestled with the idea of being a messenger of God. Fear gripped my heart because I felt that my knowledge of God was extremely limited and I was not worthy as an individual to take on the task of telling people about Jesus Christ. A part of me wanted to be excited but most of me thought "you are not worthy, you don't know enough." I knew that the will of God will never lead me where the grace of God will not keep me. But at the time, I did not understand that it was all about God and not about me and my weaknesses.

2. Lack of support. I was in a church but not one that had an intensive training process for those who heard the call of God on their life. I felt alone. There was no one to take me under their wing and give me the nurturing that I needed. Around the time when I was making the effort to answer the call, women were not encouraged to pursue our calling. The one woman minister in my church who I thought would have helped me fought me mentally and spiritually and made it very tough for me. She was a mean saint with a jealous, controlling spirit who was used to being in charge and did not welcome any help. One of the young men referred to her as,

---

[70] Isaiah 6:5.

"God's big sister." Sometimes I would leave church and go home and cry asking God: why does she make things so difficult for me? So there I was struggling trying to understand my calling and not realizing that the struggle I was experiencing was actually part of my preparation for the ministry.

3. Fear of rejection. I wanted to be accepted, and encouraged, but at that time, I did not know of many women preachers who were celebrated by their pastors. I often followed my pastor to revivals as a supporter. Sometimes I was asked to accompany the other preachers to the pulpit but most of the times I was not. But if a male preacher came in even after the service had begun, everything would stop while he was graciously ushered to the pulpit. I did not know whether to be humbled or insulted.

Those were some of my struggles early on in ministry while answering the call. Presently I have grown and realized through the work and comfort of the Holy Spirit that it is not about where I serve or who accepts me or not. It is about the glorious work of the ministry of Jesus Christ who has called me and is preparing me for such a time as this. There were many struggles. I am not saying that I have completely overcome them, but I have come to realize that answering the call requires sacrifice of self and submission to the One who calls, equips and ordains, God our Father in heaven.

I am thankful for the opportunity that God afforded me to study at Beulah Heights University. Although my formal biblical studies started at McAfee School of Theology, my first major spiritual encounters came while I was pursing a Masters of Divinity degree at Beulah Heights University. I enrolled in classes designed to help me to become stronger spiritually and in the knowledge of the Word of God. I took a class in Pastoral Care, for example, thinking it would prepare me to help others but it ended up helping me. I am thankful for the interactions with my professors and fellow-students at Beulah Heights University as the Lord prepares for ministry.

I admonish you, my dear friends, that God has a call on your life. He needs you more now than ever. Do not let fear and doubt set in and fail to go forth. You have a voice—a nurturing, loving voice that needs to be heard. Many are broken, troubled, despondent and empty, searching for peace, comfort and strength. It is imperative that you answer the call and get about your Father's business. You may have to endure difficulties but God will keep you through all of it. He promised never to leave you or forsake you and He is faithful concerning His promises. When Jesus came to earth, He called women to salvation, to healing, to restoration, to witness. He is still calling. My sister it is time to answer the call. I beg of you to answer the call.

Mission Possible
By Christine Hameed

My life's mission is to avail myself to the call, need and cry of those who have been affected by a quagmire of negative circumstances in life. On a daily basis, I seek to address the needs of those I come in contact with—the least, the last, and the lost. The fact that God has given us the power and authority to work within his glorious kingdom is wonderful in itself. Through the years, I have served God by meeting both the material and non-material needs of others. It is not an impossible task, however, it is sometimes challenging. When I know whose authority I am working within; I know I can do all things through Christ.

***

As a young girl, I wanted to be a missionary. It was obvious that God had placed this desire in me. In my youth, I saw my grandmother and mother cultivate gardens to provide fresh vegetables for our family and several families who lived around us. I wondered why we were growing food and giving it away. My grandmother instilled in me the importance of taking care of our family and those within our community. "We are our brother's keeper," she said. "You will understand it better by and by." That was the seed that was planted within me; I had more to think about in life than just myself. From that point on, I always offered to share with others anything I had. It led to a life of personal sacrifice and service to my community.

I realized early on that I had the passion for helping others, but I could not connect the dots. I knew what I wanted to do, but had no knowledge base to achieve it. The importance of a formal education was not emphasized in my family. At this point, I realized that the only obstacle that stood in my way was education. I had some of the same issues as the individuals I was trying to help. I knew Christ had called me, but I needed to become empowered in knowledge.

I was excited when I finally enrolled in Beulah Heights University (then Beulah Heights Bible College) and found out that there was a degree which held all of the components that I needed. The Community and Global Economic Development degree was the missing link in my ministry; it could propel me to a global arena. Now the true missionary was in the making. I could evangelize, lead people to Christ, and empower them in areas that would help sustain their economic development. What a gift! My confidence level increased as I acquired a strong knowledge base and rich skill-sets within my ministry. Today, I have completed my Bachelor's Degree in Community and Global Economic Development. I acquired my Masters in Leadership and Administration in May of 2009, and plan to graduate with my Masters of Divinity in May 2011. It has been a roller coaster ride with many personal challenges, but the education arm of my journey has been quite fulfilling. I now have the skills and the ability to apply what I have learned to make a contribution towards the economic empowerment of communities within a global context.

***

Let me not jump too far ahead. I must cover some basic steps that I took. In the beginning I volunteered with organizations such as the American Red Cross, DeKalb Medical Reserve, Ambassadors of DeKalb County, Atlanta Food Bank, and various shelters throughout metropolitan

Atlanta. By networking with these organizations, I was able to acquire food and shelter for many needy people around the city.

I was criticized by my family and friends who thought my efforts should have been put towards earning a salary. Since I knew this was my calling, I relentlessly continued doing my volunteer work.

I soon learned that volunteering brings rewards down the road. It was important for me to be exposed to well established organizations that focus on community development. This gave me first-hand knowledge of how to structure, manage, and organize a community based organization. Volunteering also gave me practical experience on how to deal with some important economic development concerns that I would tackle later on in my own ministry.

Matthew 28:18-20 is the mission statement that has been readily accepted as the mandate for evangelism. However, the mission statement that relates to my ministry is:

> *...for I was hungry and you gave Me food; I was thirsty and you gave Me drink; I was a stranger and you took Me in; I was naked and you clothed Me; I was sick and you visited Me; I was in prison and you came to Me.' "Then the righteous will answer Him, saying, 'Lord, when did we see You hungry and feed You, or thirsty and give You drink? When did we see You a stranger and take You in, or naked and clothe You? Or when did we see You sick, or in prison, and come to You?' And the King will answer and say to them, 'Assuredly, I say to you, inasmuch as you did it to one of the least of these My brethren, you did it to Me.'* [71]

---

[71] Mark 25:35-40.

This narrative gives us the power and authority to address the spiritual and material needs of those around us. I finally realized who I was in Christ, and the power, grace, and mercy that I was empowered with to do His work. With a handle on education, a network of individuals, and organizations by my side, I felt propelled to march on, and see what the end might be.

***

Five days after receiving my Bachelor's degree, I was sitting in the parking lot of my auto insurance company after scraping up the money to pay my bill. I was having a conversation with God when my cell phone rang. It was a government agency offering me a job as a Community Disaster Reservist. The job would involve providing assistance in disasters of all types—working alongside FEMA—as well as providing financial assistance to communities in need. The Human Resource Officer gave me information about the job and an itinerary to travel to Sacramento for training. God had rewarded me in the area of my calling.

***

Eight years ago, I could see how things were beginning to become difficult for the ordinary person. The economy began to change drastically after the tragedies of September 11th. Money, food, jobs and other resources began to dry up. I could see a definite need for my ministry. With a vision, business plan, and possibilities in hand, I developed my ministry, prophetically named "Arise and Shine", to enable communities to become self-sufficient.

It is my intention to extend my local ministry to the global arena. The two can easily work hand in hand. I learned that we are a blessed nation. Even though the economy is down, we still have a wealth of resources that are stored or discarded. These resources can be transferred to developing countries in need. My contacts have been established in Tanzania, where I feel God has called me to work. In college I met an individual who lives there, and we have communicated and are committed to working together. Our desire is to build a children's home outside the capital city. I am looking forward to traveling to Tanzania to become better acquainted with the community and their needs.

Beyond the children's home, my ministry will focus on micro-enterprise development. This will enable the community, mainly women, to start small businesses in order to become self-sufficient. A group of women in the rural area could buy a goat, for example, with a small amount of money. The sale of the milk of that goat will enable them to buy another goat, and so on. This can be done throughout an entire area, attracting churches and other groups. Through this concept, income will be generated. This could enable them to provide food, clothing, school fees, and medical care for their families. In many cases, micro-finance has enabled small communities to build schools and clinics, provide piped water, and so on. My ministry will provide small loans to members of the community to jumpstart their businesses. Eventually, the community members will pay back their loans and continue to expand. This approach to social and economic development is in line with *Ujamaa* (meaning familyhood or brotherhood in Kiswahili) which is a widespread practice in Tanzania. It is the idea of collective problem solving for the benefit of the entire community. Through *Ujamaa* we become our brother's keeper.

I am excited about what God is doing through my ministry! I would like to thank a few people who were instrumental in my development over the years. Dr. Betty

Palmer, the Chair of the Department of Leadership Studies at Beulah Heights University, exposed me to the principles of micro-finance as a strategy to empower local communities at home and abroad; and Dr. Doug Chatham, former Chair of the Graduate Studies Department at Beulah Height University, introduced me to the importance of being sensitive to the needs of communities, rather than imposing my own cultural values. I also thank two other faculty members at Beulah Heights University: Dr. John Nash, who kept me girded up in prayer, and Dr. Mae Alice Reggy who exposed me to the complexities of cross-cultural ministry.

The Bible says *"He who continually goes forth weeping, Bearing seed for sowing, Shall doubtless come again with rejoicing, Bringing his sheaves with him."*[72] Those who help me carry the seeds will rejoice at the time of completion. With God's help, these efforts will be successful. The workers are in place. The plan is developed, and the harvest is in full view. With the help of the Lord this mission is possible!

---

[72] Psalms 126:6.

About the Authors

Natalie Brannon-Lipede, a native of Atlanta, Georgia., has served as founding pastor of the Rock Christian Center in Lithonia, Georgia since January 2010. She was ordained into ministry in February, 1994 in Albany, Georgia by Bishop Q.S. Caldwell Th.D. under Celebration of Praise Ministries Inc. Over the years, she has served as Sunday school teacher, Vacation Bible School Coordinator, Assistant Music and Arts Director; and Intercessor. For over fourteen years, she also served alongside her mother, Elder Beverly Brannon, in WOMAN Outreach Ministries. In 2009 she became a National Youth President for Celebration of Praise Ministries Inc. She has been married to Minister Charles Lipede for nearly eighteen years; they are the blessed parents of three children – Patience, 15, Destiny, 12, and Nathaniel 6 years old. She is a graduate of Brenau University with an earned degree in Early Childhood Education. She is a tenured teacher of ten years and has received several awards of recognition: Outstanding Teacher Award, Diversity Award, and Parent Partnership Awards. She will graduate from Beulah Heights University in May 2011 with a Masters Degree in Biblical Studies.

Wanda Crowder has worked for the Monroe County Board of Education for the past twenty-three years. She graduated from Tift College with a BA degree in Criminal Justice. She began graduate studies at McAfee School of Theology but completed her graduate studies at Beulah Heights University where she earned a MA degree in Biblical Studies. She is presently working on a M. Div at Beulah Heights University. She attends Towaliga County Line Baptist Church where she serves as

Minister of Christian Education and also co-teaches an Adult Sunday school class with her husband Sergeant Major Jeffrey Crowder who is a full time National Guard. They have a son who is a US Marine and has served in Iraq three times. They have two daughters; one started at FVSC in 2009 and the other is a junior at Mary Persons High School in Monroe County, Georgia.

Christine Hameed was born in Chicago, transplanted to North Carolina as a young girl. She relocated to Georgia in 1970 where she joined Beulah Missionary Baptist Church and became active in the Missionary Department. Her mission work led her to become involved in the General Missionary Baptist Convention USA and acted as Vice President for the Women's Department in Atlanta's 5th District. She received a Bachelors Degree in Community and Global Economic Development and a Masters in Community and Global Economic Development from Beulah Heights University in 2007. She is the mother of one daughter, Tonya, and son-in-law, Duane Jackson, who are both in the ministry. She has two grandchildren, Maya and Madison, both close to her heart. With a burning desire for mission work, she has decided to venture into ground-breaking areas of ministry both locally and abroad. She is particularly excited about her future in the development of economic concerns of women in East Africa.

Patricia J. Jones has worked at Atlanta Union Mission for the past six years. She graduated from the University of Kentucky with a BA degree in Social Work. She is presently completing her MA degree in Biblical Studies at Beulah Heights University. She attends Zion Missionary Baptist Church under the Pastoral care of Rev. Frank Lewis. Ms. Jones has two sons and a daughter. One son is a pastor living in Louisville,

Kentucky and her other son lives in Roswell GA. Her daughter attends Independence High School in Alpharetta, Georgia. She is the proud grandmother of two grandsons and a granddaughter.

Rebecca Manning has worked with the Department of Veteran Affairs since 2000. She has served as a supervisor in the Loan Guaranty Division of the Atlanta Regional Office. She has worked as a government employee for 19 years. In 2008, she was selected to participate in the Agency's prestigious, Leadership and Development Program. She attended Merced College and financial industry training classes. She earned an AA degree in Biblical studies as well as a BA in Biblical Studies from Beulah Heights University. She is currently pursuing a MA degree in Leadership and Organization from Beulah Heights University. She serves in the Women's Mentoring Ministry and Hospitality Ministry at Mount Paran Church of God. Dr David Cooper is her pastor. She is married to Ronald T. Manning, retired U.S. army. They have a blended family of five children.

T. G. Monroy is a wife, mother, and ordained minister in the metro Atlanta area. Her career as a licensed real estate broker/owner of Tracy Monroy & Associates Realty has been an avenue for "market place ministry" over the years used for servant leadership. Minister Monroy is a life learner having earned an Associate of Arts in Leadership and Administration (2005 Beulah Heights Bible College); Bachelor of Arts in Leadership and Administration (2007) Beulah Heights University), Summa Cum Laude; and a Master of Divinity (2010, ITC), with Honors. Minister Monroy is also an active member of various honor societies: Delta Epsilon Chi, Beta Eta Beta Kappa, and Theta Phi International. Currently, she serves as an associate minister at Zion Hill Baptist Church and teaches Church school on Saturday mornings. Minister Monroy has traveled domestically and internationally finding a passion for missionary and evangelist work believing God's act of creation is an act of liberation.

Beverly Ponder began her years of study at Jersey City State College located in Jersey City, New Jersey studying Criminal Justice/Sociology. She has been a certified paralegal for the last twenty-two years. After relocating to Georgia in 1999, she began her Biblical Studies at the Beulah Heights University where she has earned her Associates and Bachelor in Biblical Education, and Masters in Biblical Studies. She is presently working on her Doctor of Divinity Degree. She is the Executive Director, City of Rest, a forth coming non-profit transitional home for women while she volunteers as a Drug and Alcohol Counselor with Jesus Set the Captive Free, a non-profit transitional home for men. She attends New Canaan Word of God Ministries where she serves as coordination of the Ministerial Alliances Ministry, as well as associate to the pastor. Her pastor is Steven D King. She is married to Ernest Ponder. She has five sons and thirty-five grandchildren.

Anyango E. Reggy was born in Washington D.C. and raised in Kenya where her family moved during her early infancy. She returned to the United States to pursue her Bachelor of Arts in Psychology (with an emphasis on International Communications) from Eastern University; a Master of Arts in International Affairs and Development from Clark Atlanta University; and a Ph.D. in African Studies from Howard University. She has been actively involved in education and advocacy on international issues with a particular focus on women and youth. She has written and presented extensively on issues of gender equality and conflict resolution in Africa. She has worked with the Academic Study Associate program to develop the Leaders for Social Change program for Yale University and Stanford University. She also served as the Coordinator of the Leaders for Social Change program at Yale University. She worked with Sesame Workshop as the Educational Content Specialist for Sub-Saharan Africa and Pakistan. Presently, she serves on the Adjunct Faculty at Beulah Heights University teaching courses on gender development, and conflict management. She is also teaching at the National University of Rwanda's Center for Conflict Management.

About the Editor

Mae Alice Reggy was born and raised in New Jersey. She earned a BA degree from Douglass College, Rutgers University, an MA degree from Howard University, and a Ph.D. from University of Maryland. She was based in Nairobi, Kenya for more than twenty-seven years, working with the United Bible Societies as Literacy Consultant for 38 African countries and serving as member of the Collective Consultation on Literacy & Education for All. She has written several books including Widows: The Challenges and the Choices (1999) and Christian Ethics (2010). She contributed to the *Women's Study New Testament* (1998), the *Africa Bible Commentary* (2006), and *Sisters on the Journey* (2010). She presently serves on the Adjunct Faculty at Beulah Heights University in Atlanta, Georgia, and as Visiting Lecturer at the Monrovia Bible College in Liberia, West Africa. She also serves the ministerial team at Total Grace Christian Center in Decatur, Georgia.

CPSIA information can be obtained at www.ICGtesting.com
Printed in the USA
BVOW09s2225231014

372174BV00017B/121/P